AF540622

ENGINEERING FOR AGRICULTURAL DRAINAGE

By

Dr. H. Shivanna

Professor & Head

Deptt. of Forest Biology & Tree Improvement

College of Forestry

SIRSI, Uttar Kannada

Karnataka

(India)

DISCOVERY PUBLISHING HOUSE PVT. LTD.

NEW DELHI-110 002

Published by:
Tilak Wasan
DISCOVERY PUBLISHING HOUSE PVT. LTD.
4383/4B, Ansari Road, Darya Ganj
New Delhi-110 002 (India)
Phone : +91-11-23279245, 43596064-65
Fax : +91-11-23253475
E-mail : parul.wasan@gmail.com
discoverypublishinghouse@gmail.com
web : www.discoverypublishinggroup.com

First Edition: **2013**

ISBN: 978-93-5056-260-4

Engineering for Agricultural Drainage

Printed at:
Aditi Fine Art Press
Delhi

Preface

Surface drainage improvements are designed for dual purposes: to minimize crop damage resulting from water ponding on the soil surface following a rainfall event, and to control runoff without causing erosion. It can affect the water-table by reducing the volume of water entering the soil profile. This type of improvement includes: land levelling and smoothing; the construction of surface water inlets to subsurface drains; and the construction of shallow ditches and grass waterways, which empty into open ditches and streams.

An important water quality function of wetlands is the trapping and filtering of sediment, nutrients and other pollutants that enter runoff from agricultural, construction and other rural and urban sources. Interestingly, subsurface drainage improvements, in a more limited capacity, provide some of these same water quality benefits while providing a necessary element for sustained agricultural production on a majority of Ohio's productive agricultural soils.

Environmental Control Drainage reduces surface run off by increasing the water holding capacity of the soil so erosion is dramatically decreased in many cases. During heavy rain, water is removed by being absorbed into the soil and filtering down through the soil to the drain, rather than running over a saturated surface and washing away valuable soil.

My near and dear ones encouraged me to write a book on this topic. Writing a book is not a simple task, as one have to burn midnight-oil for writing a perfect and up-to-date book. For author, it's like scaling a Mount

Everest. For a long period, I read many books on this subject at various libraries. I also search on Internet for up-to-date information. I am grateful to all resources, otherwise the publication of this wouldn't have been possible. I can't forget the king support of many librarians who personally helped me in searching a book at library. Information on Internet is vast and knowledgeable.

—Author

Contents

1 Introduction

Undoutedly, a drainage system will improve the crop yield. It gives you more control over the moisture content of the soil. With Global Positioning System (GPS), one can see the overall condition of the soil, and can check yielding patterns and improve moisture content of the soil.

AGRICULTURAL DRAINAGE SYSTEM

An agricultural drainage system is a system by which the water level on or in the soil is controlled to enhance agricultural crop production.

Agricultural drainage is the removal of excess water from the soil surface and/or soil profile of cropland, by either gravity or artificial means. The two main reasons for improving the drainage on agricultural land are for soil conservation and enhancing crop production. Research conducted in Ohio and throughout the Midwest has documented many benefits of agricultural drainage improvement.

Drainage is of two forms :

1. Surface drainage; and
2. Sub surface drainage or underground drainage.

Surface drainage (Natural system of drainage)

It may consist of open ditches that are laid out by eye judgement, leading from one wet spot to another and finally into a nala or river. This is often called natural system.

Advantages of Drainage Systems

1. Removes toxic material and disease organisms. Also, reduces soil erosion by creating better root systems.
2. Checks planting delays resulting in a longer growing season.
3. Reduces the effect of droughts and excessive water.
4. Improves aeration and the nitrogen content.

Open Ditch Drains

The pattern of ditches is regular. The method is adopted to land that has uniform slope.

Field Ditches

Field ditches for surface drains may be either narrow with nearly vertical sides or V-shaped with flat side slopes. V-shaped ditches have the advantages of being easier to cross with large machinery.

Narrow Ditches

These are most common where large farm machinery is not used.

In level areas, a collecting ditch may need to be installed at one side of the field and shallow shaped ditches are constructed to discharge into the collecting ditch. The field ditches should be laid out parallel and spaced 15 to 45 metres or more apart as required by the soil surface conditions and crop to be grown. They should be 30 to 60 cm deep depending upon the depth of the collecting ditch.

Farming operations should be parallel to the field ditches. The care that a ditch will drain satisfactorily depends up on how quickly water runs into the ditch how much rain falls on the land, slope, and the condition of the soil and plant cover.

Sub-surface or Under Ground Drainage

A sub-surface or underground drainage will remove excess soil water. It percolates in to themselves, just like open drains. These underground drains afford the utility that the surface of the field is not cut off, no wastage of lad and do not interfere with farm operations. On the other hand, they are costly to lie and are useless in slowly permeable clay soils.

Underground drains may be classified as:

1. Tile drain

It consists of digging a narrow trench, placing short section of tiles at the bottom and covering the tiles with earth. The loose joints between two section of the tiles serve as a opening where drainage water may enter into the drainage system. Water moves by gravity into the joins between tiles and through tile walls.

Porous tile gives no better drainage than tiles that water does not percolate and porous tile can easily broken or crushed. the drains are two types of tiles in use. Tile should be always placed at least 75 cm deep to prevent breakage by heavy machinery.

2. Box drains

Instead of pipes, underground drains may be made in V-shaped cut or trench, sides of which are reverted with soil, restoring the surface of the field. Depth may be 90 cm below ground.

3. Rubble drains

A somewhat equally substitute for tile drains is made by cutting narrow V-shaped drains or rectangular in section, as for box drains, filling them up with rough stones large and small and then covering the whole up with soil level with surface field soil. Depth may be 90 cm.

4. Mole drains

They are often used in clay, clay loam soils. A moling machine is one that draws a bullet nosed cylinder; usually 10-15 cm in diameter is therefore formed. A mole drain should be at least 75 cm below the surface to prevent closing of the holes by compaction from farming operations. Mole drains are extremely used in Europe.

5. Drainage pipe applications

The pumps are used in U.S.A. and many other countries for drainage. River bottoms, lakes and costal plains, peat lands and irrigated lands are the main types of lands reclaimed by pump drainage. The subsequent must be sufficiently permeable for the ground water to move to the pipes enough for effective pumping.

Functions of the Field Drainage

The function of the field drainage system is to control the water table, whereas the function of the main drainage system is to collect, transport, and dispose of the water through an outfall or outlet. In some instances one makes an additional distinction between collector and main drainage systems.

Field drainage systems are differentiated in surface and sub-surface field drainage systems.

Sometimes like in irrigated, submerged rice fields, a form of temporary drainage is required whereby the drainage system is allowed to function on certain occasions only (e.g. during the harvest period). If allowed to function continuously, excessive quantities of water would be lost. Such a system is therefore called a checked, or controlled, drainage system.

However, the drainage system is meant to function as regularly as possible to prevent undue water logging at any time and one employs a regular drainage system. In literature, this is sometimes also called a "relief drainage system".

The use of surface and subsurface drainage improvements is not limited to agricultural lands. Many residential homes use subsurface drainage systems, similar to those used in agriculture, to prevent water damage to foundations and basements. Golf courses make extensive use of both surface and sub-surface drains. Houses, streets and buildings in urban areas depend heavily on surface and subsurface drainage systems for protection. These generally are a combination of plastic or metal gutters, and concrete pipes or channels.

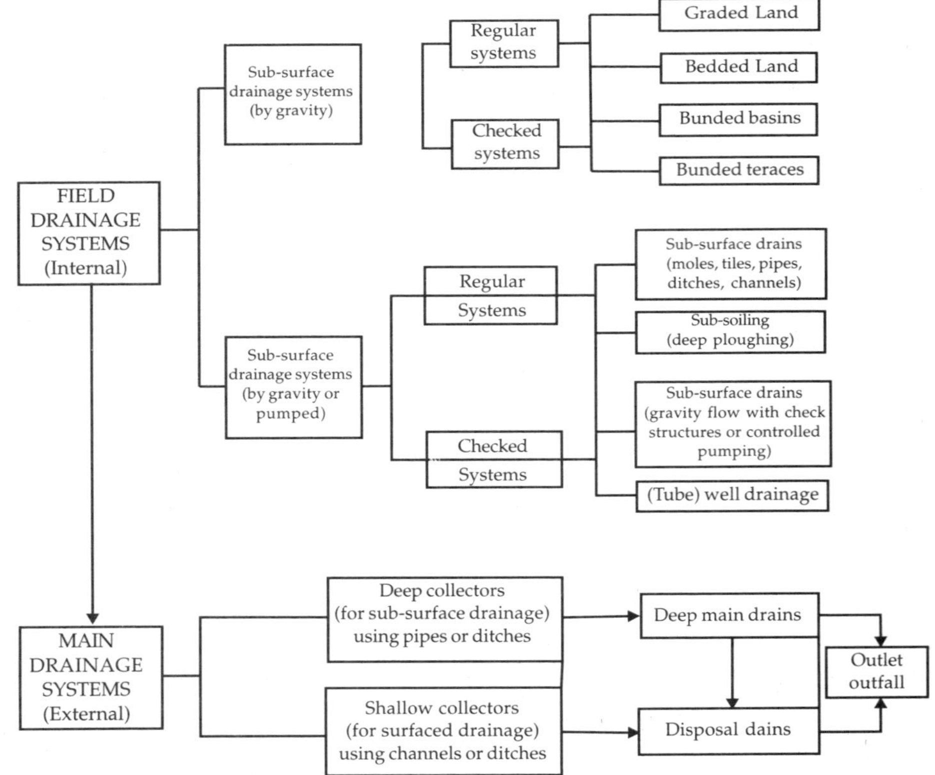

Fig. 1.1: Classification of agricultural drainage systems

Figure 1.1 classifies the various types of drainage systems. It shows the field (or internal) and the main (or external) systems.

SURFACE DRAINAGE SYSTEMS

The regular surface drainage systems, which start functioning as soon as there is an excess of rainfall or irrigation, operate entirely by gravity. They consist of reshaped or reformed land surfaces and can be divided into:

- *Bedded systems:* It is used in flat lands for crops other than rice; and
- *Graded systems:* It is used in sloping land for crops other than rice.

The bedded and graded systems may have ridges and furrows. The checked surface drainage systems consist of check gates placed in the embankments surrounding flat basins, such as those used for rice fields in flat lands. These fields are usually submerged and only need to be drained on certain occasions like at harvest time. Checked surface drainage systems are also found in terraced lands used for rice.

In literature, not much information can be found on the relations between the various regular surface field drainage systems, the reduction in the degree of waterlogging, and the agricultural or environmental effects. It is therefore difficult to develop sound agricultural criteria for the regular surface field drainage systems. Most of the known criteria for these systems concern the efficiency of the techniques of land leveling and earthmoving.

Similarly, agricultural criteria for checked surface drainage systems are not very well-known.

Sub-surface Drainage Systems

Surface drainage improvements are designed for two purposes: to minimize crop damage resulting from water ponding on the soil surface following a rainfall event, and to control runoff without causing erosion. Surface drainage can affect the water-table by reducing the volume of water entering the soil profile. This type of improvement includes: land leveling and smoothing; the construction of surface water inlets to subsurface drains; and the construction of shallow ditches and grass waterways, which empty into open ditches and streams.

Land smoothing or levelling is a water management practice designed to remove soil from high spots in a field, and/or fill low spots and depressions where water may pond. Shallow ditches may be constructed to divert excess water to grass waterways and open ditches, which often empty into existing surface water bodies.

Some disadvantages of surface drainage improvements exist. First, these improvements require annual mainte-nance and must be carefully designed to ensure that erosion is controlled. Second, extensive earthmoving activities are expensive, and land grading might expose less fertile and less productive subsoils. Further, open ditches may interfere with moving farm equipment across a field.

The objective of subsurface drainage is to drain excess water from the plant root zone of the soil profile by artificially lowering the water-table level. Subsurface drainage improvement is designed to control the water-table level through a series of drainage pipes (or tubing) that are installed below the soil surface, usually just below the root zone. For Ohio conditions, subsurface drainpipe is typically installed at a depth of 30 to 40 inches, and at a spacing of 20 to 80 feet. The subsurface drainage network generally outlets to an open ditch or stream. Subsurface drainage improvement requires some minor maintenance of the outlets and outlet ditches. For the same amount of treated acreage, subsurface drainage improvements generally are more expensive to construct than surface drainage improvements.

Whether the drainage improvement is surface, subsurface or a combination of both, the main objective is to remove excess water quickly and safely to reduce the potential for crop damage. In a situation where water is ponded on the soil surface immediately following a rainfall event, a general rule of thumb for most agricultural crops grown in Ohio is to lower the water table to 10 to 12 inches below the soil surface within a 24-hour period, and 12 to 18 inches below the soil surface within a 48-hour period. Properly draining excess water from the soil profile where plant roots grow helps aerate the soil and reduces the potential for damage to the roots of growing crops. Further, proper drainage will produce soil conditions more favorable for conducting farming operations. In states that depend heavily on irrigation, subsurface drainage is often used to prevent harmful buildup of salt in the soil.

Like the surface field drainage systems, the subsurface field drainage systems can also be differentiated in regular systems and checked (controlled) systems.

Fig. 1.2: Mug and sole drain which was widely used in Scotland during 18th Century

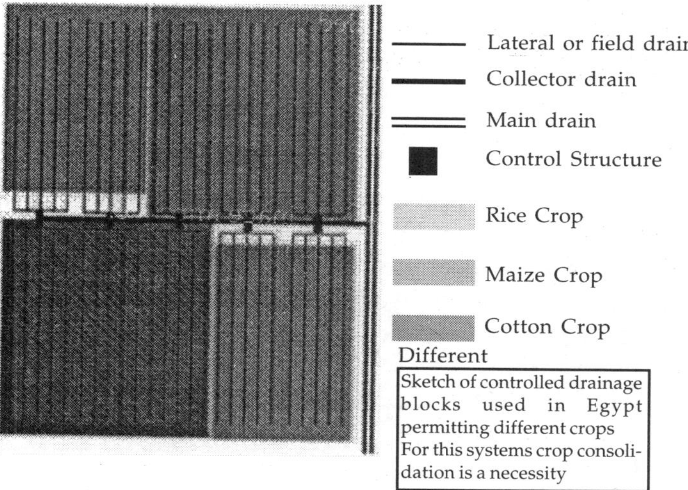

Fig. 1.3: Controlled drainage system

When the drain discharge takes place entirely by gravity, both types of subsurface systems have much in common, except that the checked systems have control gates that can be opened and closed according to need. They can save much irrigation water. A checked drainage system also reduces the discharge through the main drainage system, thereby reducing construction costs.

When the discharge takes place by pumping, the drainage can be checked simply by not operating the pumps or by reducing the pumping time. In northwestern India, this practice has increased the irrigation efficiency and reduced the quantity of irrigation water needed, and has not led to any undue salinization.

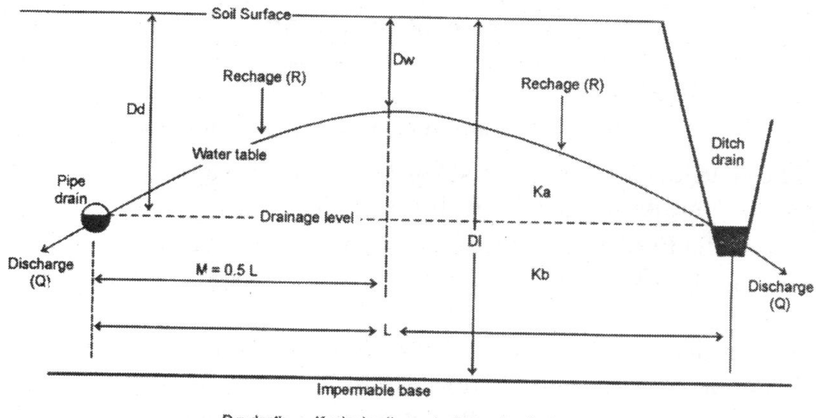

Fig. 1.4: Parameters of horizontal drainage

The subsurface field drainage systems consist of horizontal or slightly sloping channels made in the soil; they can be open ditches, trenches, filled with brushwood and a soil cap, filled with stones and a soil cap, buried pipe drains, tile drains, or mole drains, but they can also consist of a series of wells.

Modern buried pipe drains often consist of corrugated, flexible, and perforated plastic (PE or PVC) pipe lines wrapped with an envelope or filter material to improve the permeability around the pipes and to prevent entry of soil particles, which is especially important in fine sandy and silty soils. The surround may consist of synthetic fibre (geo textile).

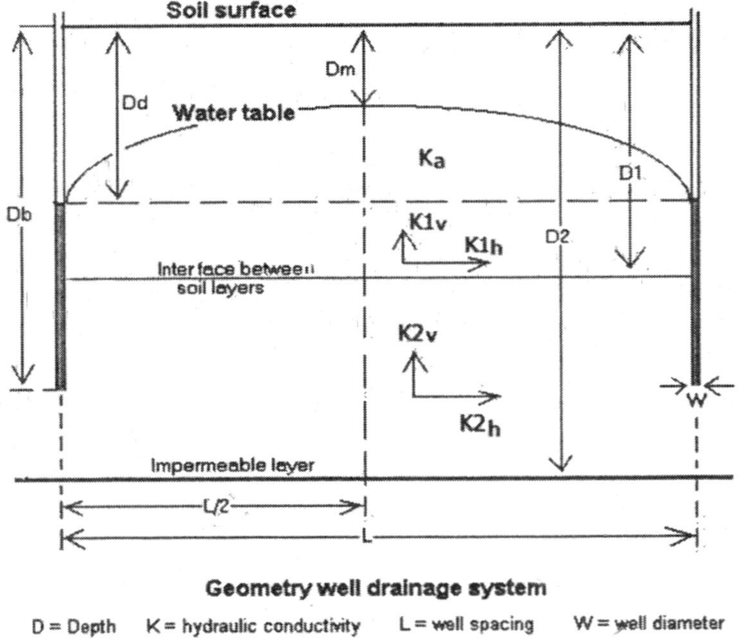

Fig. 1.5: Parameters of vertical drainage

The field drains (or laterals) discharge their water into the collector or main system either by gravity or by pumping.

The wells (which may be open dug wells or tube wells) have normally to be pumped, but sometimes they are connected to drains for discharge by gravity.

Subsurface drainage by wells is often referred to as vertical drainage, and drainage by channels as horizontal drainage, but it is more clear to speak of "field drainage by wells" and "field drainage by ditches or pipes" respectively.

In some instances, subsurface drainage can be achieved simply by breaking up slowly permeable soil layers by deep plowing (sub-soiling), provided that the underground has sufficient natural drainage. In other instances, a combination of sub-soiling and subsurface drains may solve the problem.

Main Drainage Systems

The main drainage systems consist of deep or shallow collectors, and main drains or disposal drains.

Deep collector drains are required for subsurface field drainage systems, whereas shallow collector drains are used for surface field drainage systems, but they can also be used for pumped subsurface systems. The deep collectors may consist of open ditches or buried pipe lines.

Fig. 1.6: Deep collector drain

The terms 'deep collectors and shallow collectors' refer rather to the depth of the water level in the collector below the soil surface than to the depth of the bottom of the collector. The bottom depth is determined both by the depth of the water level and by the required discharge capacity.

The deep collectors may either discharge their water into deep main drains which are drains that do not receive water directly from field drains, but only from collectors, or their water may be pumped into a disposal drain.

Disposal drains are main drains in which the depth of the water level below the soil surface is not bound to a minimum, and the water level may even be above the soil surface, provided that embankments are made to prevent inundation. It can serve both subsurface and surface field drainage systems.

Deep main drains can gradually become disposal drains if they are given a smaller gradient than the land slope along the drain. The technical criteria applicable to main drainage systems depend on the hydrological situation and on the type of system.

Main Drainage Outlet

The final point of a main drainage system is the gravity outlet structure or the pumping station.

Applications

Surface drainage systems are usually applied in relatively flat lands that have soils with a low or medium infiltration capacity, or in lands with high-intensity rainfalls that exceed the normal infiltration capacity, so that frequent waterlogging occurs on the soil surface. Subsurface drainage systems are used when the drainage problem is mainly that of shallow water tables. When both surface and subsurface waterlogging occur, a combined surface/ subsurface drainage system is required.

Sometimes, a subsurface drainage system is installed in soils with a low infiltration capacity, where a surface drainage problem may improve the soil structure and the infiltration capacity so greatly that a surface drainage system is no longer required.

Applications

Surface drainage systems are usually applied in relatively flat lands that have soils with a low o r medium infiltration capacity, or in lands with high-intensity rainfalls that exceed the normal infiltration capacity, so that frequent waterlogging occurs on the soil surface.

Subsurface drainage systems are used when the drainage problem is mainly that of shallow watertables. When both surface and subsurface waterlogging occur, a combined surface/subsurface drainage system is required. Sometimes, a subsurface drainage system installed in soils with a low infiltration capacity and a surface drainage problem improves the soil structure and the infiltration capacity so greatly that a surface drainage system is no longer required. On the other hand, it can also happen that a surface drainage system diminishes the recharge of the groundwater to such a n extent that the subsurface drainage problem is considerably reduced or even eliminated.

The choice between a subsurface drainage system by pipes and ditches or by tubewells is more a matter of technical criteria and costs than of agricultural criteria, because both types of systems can be designed to meet the same agricultural criteria and achieve the same benefits.

Usually, pipe drains or ditches are preferable to wells. However, when the soil consists of a poorly permeable top layer several metres thick, overlying a rapidly permeable and deep subsoil, wells may be a better option, because the drain spacing required for pipes or ditches would be very narrow whereas the well spacing can be very wide.

When the land needs a subsurface drainage system, but saline groundwater is present at great depth, it is better to employ a shallow, closely-spaced system of pipes or ditches instead of a deep, widely-spaced system. The reason is that the deeper systems produce a more salty effluent than the shallow systems. Environmental criteria may then prohibit the use of the deeper systems.

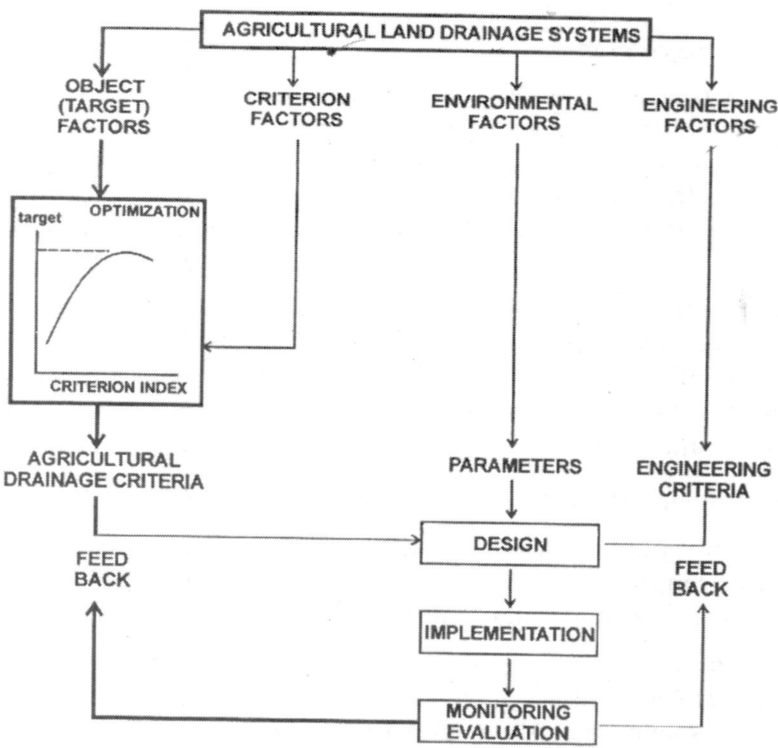

Fig. 1.7: Drainage design procedures

In some drainage projects, one may find that only main drainage systems are envisaged. The agricultural and is then still likely to suffer from field drainage problems. In other cases, one may find that field drainage systems are ineffective because there is no main drainage system. Ineither of these cases, the installation of an incomplete drainage system is not recommended.

On the other hand, it can also happen that a surface drainage system diminishes the recharge of the groundwater to such an extent that the subsurface drainage problem is considerably reduced or even eliminated.

The choice between a subsurface drainage system by pipes and ditches or by tube wells is more a matter of technical criteria and costs than of agricultural criteria, because both types of systems can be designed to meet the same agricultural criteria and achieve the same benefits.

Usually, pipe drains or ditches are preferable to wells. However, when the soil consists of a poorly permeable top layer several meters thick, overlying a rapidly permeable and deep subsoil, wells may be a better option, because the drain spacing required for pipes or ditches would be considerably smaller than the spacing for wells.

Why Deeper Systems

When the land needs a subsurface drainage system, but saline groundwater is present at great depth, it is better to employ a shallow, closely spaced system of pipes or ditches instead of a deep, widely spaced system. The reason is that the deeper systems produce a more salty effluent than the shallow systems. Environmental concerns may then stop the use of the deeper systems.

In some drainage projects, one may find that only main drainage systems are envisaged. The agricultural land is then still likely to suffer from field drainage problems. In other cases, one may find that field drainage systems are ineffective because there is no adequate main drainage system. In either case, the installation of drainage systems is not recommended.

Nature of Agricultural Drainage in Ohio: A Case Study

Currently, public concern has increased about the nature of agricultural drainage, and the impact of agricultural drainage improvements on the quality of Ohio's water resources and environment.

Agriculture is Ohio's largest industry as much of the state is characterized by fertile, flat soils and adequate rainfall, crop production occurs on 45 per cent of Ohio's land area. About 55 per cent of Ohio's agricultural soils need drainage improvement to minimize soil erosion, excess soil-water conditions in the plant root zone, and unfavorable field conditions for farm equipment in the spring and fall. Ohio's agricultural drainage needs are very similar to those in states such as Arkansas, Florida, Indiana, Illinois and Louisiana. Nationally, drainage improvement is required on more than 20 per cent of US cropland (approximately 110 out of 421 million acres).

Maintaining existing water management improvements is quite important because proper management of the soil, and soil water, is required to sustain production and profitability on agricultural soils.

Healthier Environment for Plant Growth

In Ohio, most agricultural producers improve the drainage on their land to help create a healthier environ-ment for plant growth and to provide drier field conditions so farm equipment can access the farm field throughout the crop production season.

Healthy, productive plants have the potential to produce greater yields and more food. Also, research in Ohio has shown that agricultural drainage improvement can help reduce the year-to-year variability in crop yield, which helps reduce the risks associated with the production of abundant, high quality, affordable food. Improved access of farm equipment to the field provides more time for field activities, can help extend the crop production season, and helps reduce crop damage at harvest.

Types of Improvements

In Ohio, the two primary types of agricultural drainage improvement are surface and subsurface. Many times a land owner installs a combination of these two types.

Land drainage activities have impacted Ohio's environment and water resources. Early settlers began draining Ohio's swamps in the 1850s, and today approximately 90 per cent of Ohio's wetlands have been converted to other uses. This loss is attributed to public health considerations; rural, urban and industrial development; and agriculture.

Today, however, an important distinction needs to be made between improving the drainage of wet soils presently in agricultural production and converting our "true" remaining wetlands for other purposes. True wetlands, like bogs, marshes and swamps, have saturated soil conditions over a long enough period of time during the year to maintain water-loving vegetation and wildlife habitat. These areas, once their benefit is determined, should be protected from development.

Benefits for Environment

Wetlands provide many benefits for the environment, including wildlife habitat and enhanced water quality. An important water quality function of wetlands is the trapping and filtering of sediment, nutrients and other pollutants that enter runoff from agricultural, construction and other rural and urban sources. Interestingly, subsurface drainage improvements, in a more limited capacity, provide some of these same water quality benefits while providing a necessary element for sustained agricultural production on a majority of Ohio's productive agricultural soils.

Present agricultural trends are toward more intensive use of Ohio's existing cropland, with much of the emphasis on management. Maintaining existing agricultural drainage improvements and improving the drainage on wet agricultural soils presently in agricultural production helps minimize the need for landowners to convert additional land to agricultural production. In many cases, restoration of previously converted wetlands would be impossible because of large-scale channel improvements, urbanization and Lake Erie shoreline modification. The focus should be placed on protecting existing true wetlands and establishing new wetland areas, while maintaining our highly productive agricultural areas.

Throughout Ohio and the Midwest, the removal of excess water from wet agricultural soils is essential for providing a healthy environment for crop growth, and subsequently, helps provide affordable, high-quality food. Agricultural drainage improvement is necessary to sustain agricultural production.

Factors Contributing to Excess Water Problems in Soils

The factors that contribute to excess soil water problems includes: fine soil texture; massive soil structure; low soil permeability; topography; soil compaction; restrictive geologic layer and excess precipitation.

Soil Texture

The sand, silt and clay composition of the solid mineral particles in a soil is called soil texture. For a loam soil texture, for instance, the mineral content might consist of 40 per cent clay, 30 per cent silt and 30 per cent sand.

Soil texture can have a dramatic effect on how well the soil holds water, and how easily water can move through the soil. Fine-textured soils have a large per centage of clay and silt particles. These soils generally hold water well, but drain poorly. Coarse-textured soils have a large per centage of sand or gravel particles. These soils drain well, but have poor water-holding ability.

Soil Structure

The physical arrangement of the solid mineral particles of a soil is the soil structure. A granular structure helps promote the movement of water through a soil, but a structure that is massive (lacking any distinct arrangement of soil particles) usually decreases the movement of water.

Permeability

In general terms, the relative ease with which water can move through a block of soil is soil permeability. A soil's permeability can be affected by its texture, structure, human activities, and other factors.

Topography

The shape and slope of the land surface can cause wet soil conditions, especially around depressions where water tends to accumulate. Without an outlet, the water may drain away very slowly.

Geologic Formation

The geological formation underlying a soil can impact the drainage of water from that soil. For instance, a soil could have texture and structure properties that are beneficial to the movement of water.

However, if the geologic formation underlying this soil consisted of dense clay or solid rock, it could restrict the downward movement of water, causing the soil above the formation to remain saturated during certain times of the year.

Compaction

Human activities may help create excess soil water problems. For example, operating equipment on a wet soil can compact the soil and destroy its structure.

A soil layer that is compacted will generally have no structure, and most of the voids in this layer will have been eliminated. Voids are open spaces between soil particles that can be filled with air, water, or a combination of both.

Soil water will tend to accumulate above the compacted layer because movement of water through the compacted layer is severely restricted. If the compacted layer is located at the soil surface, very little water will enter the soil and much of the water will runoff, potentially creating a flooding and/or erosion hazard.

Precipitation

Ohio's average annual precipitation is 38 inches, based on a 50-year period of precipitation records. Even though the distribution of precipitation across the state varies, the state receives an abundant supply of precipitation in an average year.

In an average month, most areas of the state receive two to four inches of precipitation. This amount is adequate to sustain high crop yields.

However, excessive rainfall, and/or winters with heavy snowfall, often produce excess soil water conditions. Furthermore, thunderstorms will frequently result in runoff because the rainfall rate is greater than the rate at which water can enter infiltrate into the soil.

BENEFITS OF AGRICULTURAL DRAINAGE

Drought Prevention

Good drainage promotes good root growth as crops reach for the capillary water in the soil. In a field with high water tables young plants only develop shallow root systems. When dry weather arrives shallow roots can not supply enough water to the crops. Consequently, it withers and dies. Crops in well drained soils have a better root system to reach the required water.

Fertilizer Efficiency

Good drainage makes any fertilizer work better. Increased fertilizer usage is no alternative to good drainage—they must be used hand in hand. Healthier soil increases the effectiveness of fertilizers, and at today's consistently climbing cost it is imperative that the maximum benefit is derived from every ounce supplied.

Environmental Control

Drainage reduces surface run off by increasing the water holding capacity of the soil so erosion is dramatically decreased in many cases. During heavy rain, water is removed by being absorbed into the soil and filtering down through the soil to the drain, rather than running over a saturated surface and washing away valuable soil.

Increased Quality

Good drainage contributes to quality. Regardless of the field, healthy roots support healthy crops. Well drained soil discourages plant disease. Also there is a direct relationship between drainage and crop quality. Time and Labour Savings Good drainage eliminates the need to work around and then return to wet spots. Profitability can be increased through faster field work and a reduced need for repeat operations such as reseeding spots.

Less Soil Damage

Good drainage avoids unnecessary soil damage such as compaction, smearing and crusting. Working in wet fields causes damage to soil structure which may take years to put right. Also, equipment which becomes bogged down means costly, time-consuming delays and often expensive damage to the machinery.

Cost Effectiveness

Expenditure of field drainage should be looked upon as a capital investment. It can bring benefits for many years.

Proper Functioning of Pipes

Methods are needed to not only locate buried agricultural drainage pipe, but to also determine if the pipes are functioning properly with respect to water delivery. The primary focus of this research project was to confirm the ability of ground penetrating radar (GPR) to locate buried drainage pipe, and then determine if GPR provides insight into drain line water conveyance functionality. Ground penetrating radar surveys using 250 MHz transmitter/ receiver antennas were conducted at a specially designed test plot under drained, moderately wet soil conditions (water-table below drain lines) and undrained, extremely wet soil conditions (water table above drain lines).

The test plot contained four drain lines: one a clay tile to corrugated plastic tubing (CPT) drain line that was completely open to flow; one comprised of CPT with an isolated obstruction near the midpoint, completely preventing through-flow of water; one comprised of CPT but filled with soil; and one comprised of CPT but severed near its midpoint, producing a partial obstruction to water flow.

Subsequent GPR computer modeling simulations were employed to assist with interpretation of the GPR field data. Results of the GPR field surveys indicate that given suitable shallow hydrologic conditions, GPR not only finds drainage pipes, but can also determine the position along a drain line where there is an isolated obstruction that completely blocks water flow. However, results show that a partial pipe obstruction is difficult to locate using GPR. Surprisingly, the soil-filled drain line was clearly detectable under both soil hydrologic conditions tested. The GPR computer modeling simulations indicate that soil had likely settled within the pipe, and that the GPR responses obtained at the test plot for the soil-filled pipe were responses representative of a pipe that was in fact only partially filled with soil. Overall, these research results provide valuable information for those contemplating the use of GPR to locate agricultural drainage pipes and then determine their functionality.

What is Agricultural Drainage Criterion?

It can be defined as criterion specifying the highest permissible levels of the water table, on o r in the soil, so that the agricultural benefits are not reduced by problems of waterlogging.

If the actual water levels are higher than specified by the criteria, an agricultural drainage system may have to be installed, or an already installed system may have to be improved, so that the water logging is eliminated. If, on the other hand, a drainage system has lowered water levels to a depth greater than specified by the criteria, we speak of a n over-designed system.

Besides employing agricultural drainage criteria, we also employ technical drainage criteria to minimize the costs of installing and operating the system, while maintaining the agricultural criteria, environmental drainage criteria (to minimize the environmental damage), and economic drainage criteria to maximize the net benefits.

Agricultural drainage systems' are systems which make it easier for water to flow from the land, so that agriculture can benefit from the subsequently reduced water levels. The systems can be made to ease the flow of water over the soil surface or through the underground, which leads to a distinction between 'surface drainage systems' and 'subsurface drainage systems'. Both types of systems need an internal or 'field drainage system', which lowers the water level in the field, and an external or 'main drainage system', which transports the water to the outlet.

Agricultural drainage systems do not necessarily lead to increased peak discharges. Although, this may occur, especially with surface drainage, the reduced waterlogging can lead to an increase in the storage of water on or in the soil during periods of peak rainfall, so that peak discharges are indeed reduced. A drainage engineer should see to it that the flow of water from the soil occurs as steadily a s possible instead of suddenly.

Sometimes like in irrigated, ponded rice fields, a form of temporary drainage is required whereby the drainage system is only allowed to function on certain occasions like during the harvest period. If allowed to function continuously, excessive quantities of water would be lost.

Such a system is therefore called a 'checked drainage system'. More usually, however, the drainage system should function as regularly as possible to prevent undue water logging at any time. We then speak of a 'regular drainage system'. In literature, this is sometimes also called 'relief drainage'.

The above definition of agricultural drainage systems excludes drainage systems for cities, highways, sports fields, and other non-agricultural purposes. Further it excludes natural drainage systems. Agricultural drainage systems are artificial and are only installed when the natural drainage is insufficient for a satisfactory form of agriculture. The definition also excludes such reclamation measures as 'hydraulic erosion control' (which aims rather at reducing the flow of water from the soil than enhancing it) and 'flood protection' (which does not enhance the flow of water from the soil, but aims rather at containing the water in watercourses). Nevertheless, flood protection and drainage systems are often simultaneous components of land reclamation projects. The reason is that installing drainage systems without flood protection in areas prone to inundation would be a waste of time and money.

Areas with both flood protection and drainage systems are often called 'polders'. Sometimes, a flood-control project alone suffices to cure the waterlogging. Drainage systems are then not required.

In literature, one encounters the term 'interceptor drainage'. The interception and diversion of surface waters with catch canals is common practice in watermanag-ement projects, but it is a flood-protection measure rather than a drainage measure. The interception of ground-water flowing laterally through the soil is usually not effective, because of the low velocities of groundwater flow (seldom more than 1 m/d and often much less). In the presence of a shallow impermeable layer, subsurface interceptor drains catch very little water and generally do not relieve water logging in extensive agricultural areas.

In the presence of a deep impermeable layer, the total flow of ground water can be considerable, but then it passes almost entirely underneath the subsurface interceptor drain. The upward seepage of groundwater cannot be intercepted by a single interceptor drain: here, one needs a regular drainage system.

Use of Check Gates

The checked surface drainage systems consist of check gates placed in the bunds surrounding flat basins, such as those used for rice fields in flat lands. These fields are usually submerged and only need to be drained o n certain occasions (e.g. at harvest time). Checked surface drainage systems are also found in terraced lands used for rice.

In literature, not much information can be found on the relationship between the various regular surface field drainage systems, the reduction in the degree of water logging, and the agricultural or environmental effects. It is therefore difficult to develop sound agricultural criteria for the regular surface field drainage systems.

Most of the known criteria for these systems concern the efficiency of the techniques of land levelling and earthmoving. Similarly, agricultural criteria for checked surface drainage systems are not very well known.

Like the surface field drainage systems, the subsurface field drainage systems can also be differentiated in regular systems and checked systems. When the drain discharge takes place entirely by gravity, both types of subsurface systems have much in common, except that the checked systems have control gates that can be opened and closed according to need. They can save much irrigation water. A checked drainage system also reduces the discharge through the main drainage system, thereby reducing construction costs.

When the discharge takes place by pumping, the drainage can be checked simply by not operating the pumps or by reducing the pumping time. In North-West India, this practice has increased the irrigation efficiency and reduced the quantity of irrigation water needed, and has not led to any undue salinization.

The subsurface field drainage systems consist of horizontal or slightly sloping channels made in the soil; they can be open ditches, buried pipe drains, or mole drains; they can also consist of a series of wells.

The channels discharge their water into the collector or main system either by gravity or by pumping. The wells which may be open dug wells or tubewells have to be pumped, but sometimes they are connected to drains for discharge by gravity. In some instances, subsurface drainage can be achieved simply by breaking up slowly permeable soil layers by deep ploughing subsoiling, provided that the underground has sufficient natural drainage. In other instances, a combination of sub soiling and subsurface drains may solve the problem.

Subsurface drainage by wells is often referred to as 'vertical drainage', and drainage by channels as 'horizontal drainage', but it is better to speak of 'field drainage by wells', or 'field drainage by ditches or pipes'.

The main drainage systems consist of deep or shallow collectors, and main drains or disposal drains. Deep collectors are required for subsurface field drainage systems, whereas shallow collectors are used for surface field drainage systems, but they can also be used for pumped subsurface systems. The terms deep and shallow collectors refer rather to the depth of the water level in the collector below the soil surface than to the depth of the bottom of the collector. The bottom depth is determined both by the depth of the water level and by the required discharge capacity.

Disposal Drains

The deep collectors may either discharge their water into deep main drains (which are drains that do not receive water directly from field drains, but only from collectors), or their water may be pumped into a 'disposal drain'.

Disposal drains are main drains in which the depth of the water level below the soil surface is not bound to a minimum, and the water level may even be above the soil surface, provided that embankments are made to prevent inundations. Disposal drains can serve both subsurface and surface field drainage systems. Deep main drains can gradually become disposal drains if they are given a smaller gradient than the land slope along the drain. The final point of a main drainage system is the gravity outlet structure or the pumping station. The technical criteria applicable to main drainage systems depend on the hydrological situation and on the type of system.

ANALYSIS OF AGRICULTURAL DRAINAGE SYSTEMS

Objectives and Effects

The objectives of agricultural drainage systems are to reclaim and conserve land for agriculture, to increase crop yields, to permit the cultivation of more valuable crops, to allow the cultivation of more than one crop a year, and/or to reduce the costs of crop production in otherwise waterlogged land. Such objectives are met through two direct effects and a large number of indirect effects.

The direct effects of installing a drainage system in waterlogged land are:

1. A reduction in the average amount of water stored on or in the soil, inducing drier.
2. A discharge of water through the system. soil conditions and reducing waterlogging.

The direct effects are mainly determined by the hydrological conditions, the hydraulic properties of the soil, and the physical characteristics of the drainage system. The direct effects trigger a series of indirect effects. These are determined by climate, soil, crop, agricultural practices, and the social, economic and environmental conditions.

Assessing the indirect effects including the extent to which the objectives are met is therefore much more difficult, but not less important, than assessing the direct effects.

The indirect effects, which can be physical, chemical, biological, and/or hydrological, can be either positive or negative. Some examples are:

- *Positive effects owing to the drier soil conditions:* increased aeration of the soil; stabilized soil structure; higher availability of nitrogen in the soil; higher and more diversified crop production; better workability of the land; earlier planting dates; reduction of peak discharges by an increased temporary storage of water in the soil;
- *Negative effects owing to the drier soil conditions:* decomposition of organic matter; soil subsidence; acidification of potential acid sulphate soils; reduced irrigation efficiency; increased risk of drought; ecological damage;

- *The indirect effects of drier soil conditions on weeds, pests, and plant diseases:* these can be both positive and negative; the net result depends on the ecological conditions;
- *Positive effects owing to the discharge:* removal of salts or other harmful substances from the soil; availability of drainage water for various purposes; and
- *Negative effects owing to the discharge:* excessive leaching of valuable nutrients from the soil; downstream environmental damage by salty or otherwise polluted drainage water; the presence of ditches, canals, and structures impeding accessibility and interfering with other infrastructural elements of the land.

Many of the indirect effects are mutually influenced and also exert their influence on the direct effects. For example, as a result of drainage, the following may happen:

(a) The more intensive agriculture increases the evapotranspiration and consequently may reduce the discharge, unless this leads to an increased irrigation intensity;

(b) The more stable soil structure may increase the infiltration and the subsurface drain discharge, and decrease the surface runoff.

AGRICULTURAL CRITERION FACTORS AND OBJECT FUNCTIONS

In agricultural drainage, one is dealing with agricultural, environmental, engineering, economic and social aspects.

The agricultural aspects concern 'object factors' and 'criterion factors'. Object factors represent the agricultural aims that are to be achieved to the highest possible degree (maximization) through a process of optimization, yielding 'agricultural targets'. Optimizing is done with criterion factors, which are factors that are affected by the drainage system and at the same time influence the object factors.

Examples of criterion factors are the degree of water logging, the dryness or wetness of the soil, and the soil salinity.

Owing to its variation in time and space, a criterion factor can be specified in different ways. A chosen specification can be called a criterion index'. Examples of such indices are:

- The average depth of the watertable during the cropping season;
- The average depth of the watertable during the off-season;
- The exceedance frequency of the watertable over a critically high level;

- Seasonal average salinity of the rootzone;
- Salinity of the topsoil at sowing time; and
- Average, minimum, or maximum number of days that the soil is workable during a critical period.

The relationship between a n object factor and an index can be called 'object function of the index' and is also known as 'response function' or 'production function'.

The optimization procedure through the object function leads to a tolerance, or even an optimum, value of the index, which can be called as an 'agricultural drainage criterion'. It serves as an instruction to the designer of the drainage system because it stipulates the agricultural condition the system must meet to be effective (i.e. to fulfil its purpose). Also, the instruction can prevent the design and implementation of a system that is unnecessarily intensive, expensive and even detrimental.

'Environmental factors' are factors representing the given natural or hydrological conditions under which the system has to function. Examples of these factors are irrigation, rainfall, the soil's hydraulic conductivity, natural surface or subsurface drainage, topography, and aquifer conditions. For design purposes, the environmental factors must be specified as 'environmental indices', in the same way as the criterion factors are specified as criterion indices.

Examples of environmental indices are the average seasonal rainfall, the extreme daily rainfall, the arithmetic or geometric mean of the hydraulic conductivity, and the variation in hydraulic conductivity with depth in the soil. Through a process of optimizing the engineering aspects, the environmental indices yield 'environmental parameters', which are fixed values of the indices, chosen as engineering or design criteria, in similarity to the agricultural criteria. Examples of such parameters are design values for rainfall, discharge, and hydraulic conductivity.

The engineering aspects include 'engineering factors' and 'engineering objectives'. The objectives usually aim at minimizing the costs, and relate to the efficiency of the drainage system. A fully efficient drainage system fulfils the agricultural criteria at the lowest possible input level of materials and finances.

The engineering factors are factors representing the technical and material components of the drainage system like the layout, the longitudinal section and the cross-section of the drains, and the kind and quality of materials. The choice of the engineering factors is specified in the tender documents produced after the design has been completed.

NATURAL DRAINAGE SYSTEM

Drainage is the process of draining the water from soaked land, through pipes, tunnels, canals, ditches and trenches. The patterns formed by streams, rivers and lakes are called as natural drainage systems. Implementation of proper drainage systems can prevent the municipal plus the rural areas from flooding. Geosynthtics are frequently used to improve performance and extend the life of drainage systems. Drainage or subsurface drainage, agricultural hydraulics, is the combination of natural and artificial systems that makes possible deep disposal of excess land. A well-drained soil occurs naturally when the water table is at proper depth and the porosity is such as which will not slow down the percolation of excess water.

There are various types of drainage systems present for natural resources. Dendritic drainage system is the most common form of drainage system in which, many contributing streams joined together into the tributaries to form larger rivers. Dendritic system forms V- shaped valley. As a result of that the rock will become non porous. Parallel drainage system is the type of drainage system in which the pattern caused by rivers resulting in steep slopes. Because of the steep slopes, all the streams flow in the same direction. The streams of this type are swift, straight and consist of very few tributaries.

Trellis is a type of drainage system, which is similar to that of a common garden trellis. When the river flows along a valley, smaller tributaries feeds into it from the steep slopes on the sides of the mountains. These tributaries join the river at about 90° angle. This appears like the drainage system and is the characteristic of the folded mountains pattern. Rectangular drainages develop on rocks, which are approximately uniform resistance to erosion but usually have two directions of joining at right angles.

Gradually, the streams develop along these joints and are comparatively less resistant to erosion than the bulk rock. Further this results in, joining of the streams with riverbed at right angle. The streams radiate is outwards from a central high point in the radial drainage system. The structure of the radial drainage system is like volcanoes. The radial drainage may lead a combination of radial and annular patterns. In deranged drainage system, there is no coherent pattern to the rivers and lakes. This type of drainage systems are found in the area where there has been much geological disruption occurred.

Domestic drainage systems designed to carry wastewater from a land to the main sewage network. Depending upon the age of the property, domestic drainage systems are classed in two different types, a single-stack and a two-pipe system. A two-pipe drainage systems were found in the houses built before late 1950s. It consists of the large diameter vertical soil pipe, which leads directly to the sewage network, and often runs down the outside wall of a property of all any new houses that are built with a single-stack drainage system. Unlike the two-pipe system, a large bore pipe often incorporated into the internal framework of a property. For cleaning the drainage systems the chemical unblockers are the good options but pumps or plungers can be used to clean the drainage systems.

Importance of Rainwater Drainage Systems

Property is always a great investment and generally it is quite a large one, if not your largest. If you own your own property you know how important it is to maintain it as well as you possibly can. So you must take care of it to ensure that it does not become damaged or badly kept. If you allow this to happen the value of your investment can be seriously affected and this is something that you must avoid.

One of your worst enemies as a property owner is the weather. Adverse weather conditions can cause a great deal of damage to your property if you do not have the proper equipment in place to protect it. Heavy rain is one of the most dangerous types of weather as moisture within your building can cause as huge amount of damage. Because of this having a high quality drainage system in place is absolutely paramount. These drainage systems are designed and manufactured to provide your building with the maximum amount of protection possible from heavy or constant rain fall.

As there are son many different types of drainage systems available on the current market place it can be a very difficult decision trying to pick the best one, especially if you are relatively new to the property game. There are a number of different factors that you will need to take into consideration when you are choosing your rainwater drainage system. Firstly, you will need to look at the style of building that you have.

It is absolutely important that the drainage system that you choose matches the style of your building. If it does not it can detract from the aesthetics of your building and thus affect the appeal and even the price of your home. This cannot be allowed to occur, so you must really take your time while browsing through the various drainage systems that are available to you.

There are plenty to choose from including modern and contemporary styled drainage systems and more traditional and classically styled drainage systems. This means that you should have no problem locating a system to suit both the style of you home and your own personal taste.

There are many different retailers from where you can get high quality rainwater drainage systems. You can purchase them from a number of retailers and home improvement stores on the high street and the selection within these stores is quite good.

However, the very best location to find not only the best selection but the best prices is the internet. Here you can gain access to the entire marketplace and you can also find sites and blogs that will offer you help and assistance that will indicate what the very best quality drainage systems are.

CHEST DRAINAGE SYSTEMS

Traditional Chest Drainage

In 1967, Deknatel introduced the first integrate ddisposable chest drainage unit based on the three bottle system.

Collection Chamber

At the right side of the unit is the collection chamber. The patient tubing connects thedrainage unit directly to the chest tube. Any drainagefrom the chest flows into this chamber. The collection chamber is calibrated and has a write-on surface toallow for easy measurement and recording of the time, date, and amount of drainage.

Water Seal Chamber

The middle chamber of a traditional chest drainage system is the water seal. The main purpose of thewater seal is to allow air to exit from the pleuralspace on exhalation and prevent air from enteringthe pleural cavity or mediastinum on inhalation.When the water seal chamber is filled with sterile fluidup to the 2 cm line, a 2 cm water seal is established.

To maintain an effective seal, it isimportant to keep the chest drainage unit upright atall times and to monitor the water level in the waterseal to check for evaporation. Bubbling in the water seal chamber indicates an airleak. The patient air leak meter indicates the approximate degree of air leak from the chest cavity. The meter is made up of numbered columns, labeled from 1 (low) to 7 (high). The higher the numbered column through which bubbling occurs, the greater the degree of air leak. Bydocumenting the number, the clinician can monitorair leak increase or decrease. The water seal chamber also has a calibrated manometer to measure the amount of negativepressure within the pleural cavity.

The water level in the small arm of the water seal rises asintrapleural pressure becomes more negative. If there is no air leak, the water level should rise andfall with the patient's respirations, reflecting normal pressure changes in the pleural cavity. During spontaneous respirations, the water level should riseduring inhalation and fall during exhalation. If the patient is receiving positive pressure ventilation, the oscillation will be just the opposite — the water level should fall with inhalation and rise with exhalation. This oscillation is called tidaling and is one indicatorof a patent pleural chest tube.At the top of the water seal chamber is a highnegativity float valve and high negativity relief chamber. These safety features maintain the water seal in the event of high negative pressures. Three situations can cause high negative pressure:

(*a*) The patient in respiratory distress, coughing vigorously, or crying;

(*b*) Chest tube stripping;

(*c*) Decreasing or disconnecting suction.

High negativity is indicated by rising water in the small arm of the water seal chamber. If the water rises beyond –20 cm, the high negativity float valve will rise and impede the flow of water, allowing the patient to develop as much negativity as needed for inspiration. In instances of falsely imposed high negative pressure, such as stripping chest tubes,water will continue to rise, filling the high negativity relief chamber.

The relief chamber automatically vents excessive negative pressure, thus preventing respiratory compromise from accumulated negativity.Vigorous milking or stripping can create dangerously high negative pressures. Research has documented negative pressures as high as –450 cm H_2O. Pleurevac prevents accumulation of excessive high negative pressure as discussed above; however, the transient high negative pressures created by vigorous stripping can put the patient at risk for media stinal trauma and graft trauma.

Use extreme caution and follow your hospital policy. A manual high negativity relief valve is located on top of chest drainage systems. Depressing the high negativity relief valve allows filtered air into the system, relieving negativity and allowing the waterlevel to return to baseline in the water seal. Use the high negativity relief valve with caution. If suction is not operative, or if operating on gravity drainage, depressing the high negativity relief valve can reduce negative pressure within the collection chamber to zero (atmosphere) with the resulting possibility of apneumothorax.

Wet Suction Control

The chamber on the left side of the unit is the suction control chamber. Traditional chest drainage units regulate the amount of suction by the height of a column of water in the suction control chamber. It is the height of water, not the setting of the suction source, that actually limits the amount of suction transmitted to the pleural cavity. Asuction pressure of –20cm H_2O is commonly recommended. Lower levels may be indicated forinfants and for patients with friable lung tissue, or if ordered by the physician. In a wet suction control system such as the Pleur-evac®A-7000/A-8000 series, fill the suction control chamber to the desired height with sterile fluid. Connect the short suction tubing to a suction source, and adjust the source suction to produce gentle bubbling in the suction control chamber. Increasing suction at the suction source will increase air flow through the system, but will have minimal effect on the amount of suction imposed on the chest cavity. Excessive source suction not only causes loud bubbling (which can disturb patients and caregivers), but also hastens evaporation of water from the suction control chamber. This results in a lower amount of suction applied to the patient as the level of water decreases. Self-sealing diaphragms are provided to adjust the water level in this chamber.

Dry Suction

The next step in the evolution of chest drainage units was the development of dry suction control chambers. Dry suction control systems provide many advantages: higher suction pressure levels can be achieved, set-up is easy, no continuous bubbling provides for quiet operation, and there is no fluid to evaporate which would decrease the amount of suction applied to the patient. Instead of regulating the level of suction with acolumn of water, the dry suction units are controlled by a self-compensating regulator. A dial to set the suction control setting is located on the upper leftside of each unit. To set the suction setting, rotate the dial until the red stripe appears in the semi-circular window at the prescribed suction level and clicks into place. Suction can be set at –10, –15,–20, –30, or –40 cm of water. The unit is pre-set at–20 cm of water when opened. Connect the short suction tubing or suction port tothe suction source. Source suction must be capableof delivering a minimum of 16 liters per minute (LPM) air flow. Increase suction source until the orange float appears in the suction control indicator window.

The unique design of the Pleur-evac dry suction control immediately responds to changes in patient pressure (patient air leak) or changes in suction pressure (surge/decrease at the suction source). The setting of the suction control dial determines the approximate amount of suction imposed regardless of the amountof source suction — as long as the orange float appears in the indicator window. Patient situations that may require higher suction pressures of –30 or –40 cm H_2O include: a large airleak from the lung surface, empyema or viscous pleural effusion, a reduction in pulmonary compliance, or anticipated difficulty in expansion of the pulmonary tissue to fill the hemithorax. In the presence of a large air leak, air flow through the Pleur-evac may be increased by increasing source suction, without increasing imposed negativity. It is not necessary to change the suction setting on the Pleur-evac unit to accommodate high air flows.

The suction control level can be changed at any time as prescribed by simply rotating the dial to the new suction setting. Confirm that the orange float remains in the suction control indicator window at the new suction setting. If suction setting is changed from a higher to a lower level, the patient negativity may remain at the higher level unless the negativity is relieved. Use the manual high negativity relief valve to reduce negativity to desired level. Both the wet suction and dry suction series of Pleurevachave a positive pressure relief valve that opens with increases in positive pressure, preventing pressure accumulation. Normally, air exits through the suction port. Obstruction of this route (i.e. a bed wheel rolls on top of the suction tube, orthe suction port is capped after suction discontinued) could cause accumulation of air in the system leading to tension pneumothorax. This safety feature allows venting of the positive pressure automatically, thus minimizing the risk of tension pneumothorax.

One-way Valve

No water is required to establish the one-way seal. Just connect the patient tube to the patient's thoracic catheter and the patient seal is established for patient protection. The one-way valve maintains the patient seal even if the unit is tipped over. Unlike a water seal system in which the seal may be lost when the unit is tipped, the Sahara dry seal protects the patient from atmospheric air. If air leak diagnostics are desired, the patient air leak meter must be filled to the "Fill". The fluid in the patient air leak meter is used for air leak detection as described earlier and is not a water seal. In the Pleur-evac Sahara, negative pressure exists in the collection chamber when the yes can be seen in the indicator indow. During gravity drainage before normal negative pressure has been re-established in the pleural cavity, the indicator may intermittently indicate negative pressure with patient respiration. During suction drainage, the pressure indicator should indicate a negative pressure continuously. The negative pressure indicator does not confirm drainage tube patency. Routinely check the drainage tube patency. The Pleur-evac Sahara system also has an automatic high negative pressure relief valve to limit the negative pressure to approximately –50 cm of H_2O. Amanual high negativity relief valve is also provided tovent excessive negativity as described earlier.

Gravity Drainage

Not all patients require suction. Suction may be discontinued to transport a patient; it may also be discontinued 24 hours before chest tube removal. Consult hospital policy to determine if an order is needed to institute or discontinue suction. If suction is discontinued, the suction tube or port should remain uncapped and free of obstructions to allow air to exit and minimize the possibility of tension pneumothorax.

DESIGN OF DRAINAGE SYSTEM

Drainage System

Drainage, it is the artificial or natural removal of surface and sub-surface water from an area. The agricultural soil requires the drainage for improving production and to manage the water supplies. The design of drainage system refers to geomorphology drainage system, agriculture drainage system and sustainable urban drainage system.

Geomorphology

The drainage system in the geomorphology is the pattern formed by the streams, rivers, and lakes in the particular drainage basin. The particular region is dominated by soft or hard rocks and the gradient of the land are governed by the topography of the land. In geomorphology, a drainage basin is the topographic region from there streams receives runoff, through flow, and ground water flow. The drainage basin are divided by topographic barrier from each other is called as watershed.

The watershed represents all of the stream branches that flow to some location along the stream channel. The drainage basin varies according to the size, shape and number of the drainage basin found in the area. This included in the design of drainage system.

Agricultural Drainage System

It is by which the water level or in the soil is controlled to increase the agricultural growth and yield crop production. There are three classification of agricultural drainage systems are available they are surface drainage system, subsurface drainage system, and main drainage system. The functioning of the surface drainage systems will start if there is an excess of rainfall or irrigation, operate entirely by gravity.

This consists of reshaped land surface and can be divided into Bedded systems, used in flat lands for crops other tan rice; graded systems, used in sloping the land for crops than rice. The subsurface drainage systems consist of drainage systems, it consist slightly sloping channels made in the soil; they can open ditches, trenches, filled with stones and soil cap, mole drains. The main drainage systems consist of deep or shallow collectors and main drains or disposal drains.

Sustainable Drainage Systems

The design of drainage system includes sustainable drainage system. This is sometime called as Sustainable Urban drainage systems; this is designed to reduce the potential impact of the new and existing developments in respect with surface water drainage discharges. To reproduce the natural systems is the idea behind sustainable drainage systems. This uses the effective cost with low environmental impact to drain away dirty and surface water collections, and cleaning them before allowing it released slowly back into environment, i.e. into water courses.

2 Soil
Nutrient Base for Plants

Soil is used in agriculture, where it serves as the primary nutrient base for plants; however, as demonstrated by hydroponics, it is not essential to plant growth if the soil-contained nutrients could be dissolved in a solution. The types of soil used in agriculture (among other things, such as the purported level of moisture in the soil) vary with respect to the species of plants that are cultivated.

Soil material is a critical component in the mining and construction industries. Soil serves as a foundation for most construction projects. Massive volumes of soil can be involved in surface mining, road building and dam construction. Earth sheltering is the architectural practice of using soil for external thermal mass against building walls.

Soil Resources

These are critical to the environment, as well as to food and fiber production. Soil provides minerals and water to plants. Soil absorbs rainwater and releases it later, thus preventing floods and drought. Soil cleans the water as it percolates. Soil is the habitat for many organisms: the major part of known and unknown biodiversity is in the soil, in the form of invertebrates (earthworms, woodlice, millipedes, centipedes, snails, slugs, mites, springtails, enchytraeids, nematodes, protists), bacteria, archaea, fungi and algae; and most organisms living above ground have part of them (plants) or spend part of their lifecycle (insects) belowground. Above-ground and below-ground biodiversities are tightly interconnected, making soil protection of paramount importance for any restoration or conservation plan.

The biological component of soil is an extremely important carbon sink since about 57 per cent of the biotic content is carbon. Even on desert crusts, cyanobacteria lichens and mosses capture and sequester a significant amount of carbon by photosynthesis. Poor farming and grazing methods have degraded soils and released much of this sequestered carbon to the atmosphere. Restoring the world's soils could offset some of the huge increase in greenhouse gases causing global warming while improving crop yields and reducing water needs.

Waste Management

Waste management often has a soil component. Septic drain fields treat septic tank effluent using aerobic soil processes. Landfills use soil for daily cover. Land application of wastewater relies on soil biology to aerobically treat BOD.

Organic soils, especially peat, serve as a significant fuel resource; but wide areas of peat production, such asspha-gnum bogs, are now protected because of patrimonial interest.

Both animals and humans in many cultures occasionally consume soil. It has been shown that some monkeys consume soil, together with their preferred food, in order to alleviate tannintoxicity.

Soils filter and purify water and affect its chemistry. Rain water and pooled water from ponds, lakes and rivers percolate through the soil horizons and the upper rock strata; thus becoming groundwater. Pests like viruses and pollutants, such as persistent organic pollutants chlorinated pesticides, polychlorinated biphenyls, oils hydrocarbons, heavy metals like lead, zinc, cadmium, and excess nutrients like nitrates, sulfates, phosphates are filtered out by the soil. Soil organisms metabolize them or immobilize them in theirbiomass and necromass, thereby incorporating them into stable humus. The physical integrity of soil is also a prerequisite for avoiding landslides in rugged landscapes.

The production and accumulation or degradation of organic matter and humus is greatly dependent on climate conditions. Temperature and soil moisture are the major factors in the formation or degradation of organic matter, they along with topography, determine the formation of organic soils. Soils high in organic matter tend to form under wet or cold conditions where decomposer activity is impeded by low temperature or excess moisture.

Land Degradation

Land degradation is a human-induced or natural process which impairs the capacity of land to function. Soils are the critical component in land degradation when it involves acidification, contamination, desertification, erosion or salination.

While soil acidification of alkaline soils is beneficial, it degrades land when soil acidity lowers crop productivity and increases soil vulnerability to contamination and erosion. Soils are often initially acid because their parent materials were acid and initially low in the basic cations (calcium, magnesium, potassium and sodium). Acidification occurs when these elements are removed from the soil profile by normal rainfall, or the harvesting of forest or agricultural crops. Soil acidification is accelerated by the use of acid-forming nitrogenous fertilizers and by the effects of acid precipitation.

Soil Contamination

Soil contamination at low levels is often within soil capacity to treat and assimilate. Many waste treatment processes rely on this treatment capacity. Exceeding treatment capacity can damage soil biota and limit soil function. Derelict soils occur where industrial contam-ination or other development activity damages the soil to such a degree that the land cannot be used safely or productively. Remediation of derelict soil uses principles of geology, physics, chemistry and biology to degrade, attenuate, isolate or remove soil contaminants to restore soil functions and values. Techniques include leaching, air sparging, chemical amendments, phytoremediation, bioremediation and natural attenuation.

Desertification is an environmental process of ecosystem degradation in arid and semi-arid regions, often caused by human activity. It is a common misconception that droughts cause desertification. Droughts are common in arid and semiarid lands. Well-managed lands can recover from drought when the rains return. Soil management tools include maintaining soil nutrient and organic matter levels, reduced tillage and increased cover. These practices help to control erosion and maintain productivity during periods when moisture is available. Continued land abuse during droughts, however, increases land degradation. Increased population and livestock pressure on marginal lands accelerates desertification.

Soil erosional loss is caused by wind, water, ice and movement in response to gravity. Although the processes may be simultaneous, erosion is distinguished from weathering. Erosion is an intrinsic natural process, but in many places it is increased by human land use. Poor land use practices including deforestation, over grazing and improper construction activity.

Improved management can limit erosion by using techniques like limiting disturbance during construction, avoiding construction during erosion prone periods, intercepting runoff, terrace-building, use of erosion-suppressing cover materials, and planting trees or other soil binding plants.

A serious and long-running water erosion problem occurs in China, on the middle reaches of the Yellow River and the upper reaches of the Yangtze River. From the Yellow River, over 1.6-billion tons of sediment flow each year into the ocean. The sediment originates primarily from water erosion gully erosion in the Loess Plateau region of northwest China.

Soil piping is a particular form of soil erosion that occurs below the soil surface. It is associated with levee and dam failure, as well as sink hole formation. Turbulent flow removes soil starting from the mouth of the seep flow and subsoil erosion advances upgradient. The term sand boil is used to describe the appearance of the discharging end of an active soil pipe.

Soil salination is the accumulation of free salts to such an extent that it leads to degradation of soils and vegetation. Consequences include corrosion damage, reduced plant growth, erosion due to loss of plant cover and soil structure, and water quality problems due to sedimentation. Salination occurs due to a combination of natural and human caused processes. Arid conditions favor salt accumulation. This is especially apparent when soil parent material is saline. Irrigation of arid lands is especially problematic. All irrigation water has some level of salinity. Irrigation, especially when it involves leakage from canals and over irrigation in the field, often raises the underlying water table. Rapid salination occurs when the land surface is within the capillary fringe of saline groundwater. Soil salinity control involves watertable control and flushing with higher levels of applied water in combination withtile drainage or another form of subsurface drainage.

Soil salinity models are applicable to assess the cause of soil salination and to optimize the reclamation of irrigated saline soils.

Process of Soil Compaction

In Geotechnical engineering, soil compaction is the process in which a stress applied to a soil causes densification as air is displaced from the pores between the soil grains. When stress is applied that causes densification due to water (or other liquid) being displaced from between the soil grains then Consolidation (soil), not compaction, has occurred. Normally, compaction is the result of heavy machinery compressing the soil, but it can also occur due to the passage of (e.g.) animal feet.

In Soil Science and Agronomy Soil compaction is usually a combination of both engineering compaction and consolidation, so may occur due to a lack of water in the soil, the applied stress being internal suction due to water evaporation as well as due to passage of animal feet.

Affected soils become less able to absorb rainfall, thus increasing runoff and erosion. Plants have difficulty in compacted soil because the mineral grains are pressed together, leaving little space for air and water, which are essential for root growth. Burrowing animals also find it a hostile environment, because the denser soil is more difficult to penetrate. The ability of a soil to recover from this type of compaction depends on climate, mineralogy and fauna. Soils with high shrink-swell capacity, such as Vertisols, recover quickly from compaction where moisture conditions are variable (dry spells shrink the soil, causing it to crack). But clays which do not crack as they dry cannot recover from compaction on their own unless they host ground-dwelling animals such as earthworms—the Cecil soil series is an example.

Methods to Achieve Compaction

There are several means of achieving compaction of a material. Some are more appropriate for soil compaction than others, while some techniques are only suitable for particular soils or soils in particular conditions. Some are more suited to compaction of non-soil materials such asasphalt. Generally, those that can apply significant amounts of shear as well as compressive stress, are most effective. The available techniques can be classified as:

1. *Static:* A large stress is slowly applied to the soil and then released.
2. *Impact:* The stress is applied by dropping a large mass onto the surface of the soil.
3. *Vibrating:* A stress is applied repeatedly and rapidly via a mechanically driven plate or hammer. Often combined with rolling compaction.
4. *Gyrating:* A static stress is applied and maintained in one direction while the soil is a subjected to a gyratory motion about the axis of static loading. Limited to laboratory applications.
5. *Rolling:* A heavy cylinder is rolled over the surface of the soil. Commonly used on sports pitches. Roller-compactors are often fitted with vibratory devices to enhance their ability.
6. *Kneading:* Shear is applied by alternating movement in adjacent positions. An example, combined with rolling compaction, is the 'sheepsfoot' roller used in waste compaction at landfills.

Work of Soil Compaction

Soil compaction is a vital part of the construction process. It is used for support of structural entities such as building foundations, roadways, walkways, and earth retaining structures to name a few. For a given soil type certain properties may deem it more or less desirable to perform adequately for a particular circumstance. In general, the preselected soil should have adequate strength, be relatively incompressible so that future settlement is not significant, be stable against volume change as water content or other factors vary, be durable and safe against deterioration, and possess proper permeability.

When an area is to be filled or backfilled the soil is placed in layers called lifts. The ability of the first fill layers to be properly compacted will depend on the condition of the natural material being covered. If poor material is left in place and covered over, it may compress over a long period under the weight of the earth fill, causing settelment cracks in the fill or in any structure supported by the fill.

In order to determine if the natural soil will support the first fill layers, an area can be proofrolled. Proofrolling consists of utilizing a piece heavy construction equipment (typically, heavy compaction equipment or hauling equipment) to roll across the fill site and watching for poor areas to be revealed. Poor areas will be indicated by the development of rutting or ground weaving.

To ensure adequate soil compaction is achieved, project specifications will indicate the required soil density or degree of compaction that must be achieved. These specifications are generally recommended by a geotechnical engineer in a geotechnical engineering report.

The soil type - that is, grain-size distributions, shape of the soil grains, specific gravity of soil solids, and amount and type of clay minerals present - has a great influence on the maximum dry unit weight and optimum moisture content. It also has a great influence on how the materials should be compacted in given situations.

Compaction is accomplished by use of heavy equipment. In sands and gravels, the equipment usually vibrates, to cause re-orientation of the soil particles into a denser configuration. In silts and clays, a sheepsfoot roller is frequently used, to create small zones of intense shearing, which drives air out of the soil.

Determination of adequate compaction is done by determining the *in situ* density of the soil and comparing it to the maximum density determined by a laboratory test. The most commonly used laboratory test is called the Proctor compaction test and there are two different methods in obtaining the maximum density. They are the standard Proctor and modified Proctor tests; the modified Proctor is more commonly used. For small dams, the standard Proctor may still be the reference.

Compaction and Plant Growth

Compaction of agricultural soils is a concern to many agricultural soil scientists and farmers, since soil compaction due to heavy field traffic may reduce plant growth. However, it cannot be stated that all compaction reduces plant growth. The topic is complicated, because it involves the response of the plant to the soil structure and the availability of water. Thus, it requires knowledge about the stress distribution in the soil below the applied load, and knowledge about the resulting soil deformation and shearing. Solutions to overcome compaction include tillage and the zaï-system.

How Soil Formation Begins?

Soil formation begins first with the break down of rock into regolith. Continued weathering and soil horizon development process leads to the development of a soil profile, the vertical display of soil horizons. Watch the typical progression of a soil profile then read the description below of a generic, fully developed soil.

O Horizon

At the top of the profile is the O horizon which is primarily composed of organic matter. Fresh litter is found at the surface, while at depth all signs of vegetation structure has been destroyed by decomposition. The decomposed organic matter, or humus, enriches the soil with nutrients like nitrogen, potassium, etc., aids soil structure which acts to bind particles, and enhances soil moisture retention.

A Horizon

Beneath the O horizon is the A horizon. The A horizon marks the beginning of the true mineral soil. In this horizon organic material mixes with inorganic products of weathering. The A horizon typically is dark coloured horizon due to the presence organic matter.Eluviation, the removal of inorganic and organic substances from a horizon by leaching occurs in the A horizon. Eluviation is driven by the downward movement of soil water.

E Horizon

The E horizon generally is a light-coloured horizon with eluviation being the dominant process. Leaching, or the removal of clay particles, organic matter, and/or oxides of iron and aluminum is active in this horizon. Under coniferous forests, the E horizon often has a high concentration of quartz giving the horizon an ashy-gray appearance.

B Horizon

Beneath the E horizon lies the B horizon. The B horizon is a zone of illuviation where downward moving, especially fine material, is accumulated. The accumulation of fine material leads to the creation of a dense layer in the soil.

In some soils the B horizon is enriched with calcium carbonate in the form of nodules or as a layer. This occurs when the carbonate precipitates out of downward moving soil water or from capillary action. The diagram below illustrates the effect of climate on eluviation and illuviation. Eluviation is significant in humid climates where ample precipitation exists and a surplus in the water balance occurs. Illuvial layers are found low in the soil profile.

Illuvial zones are found closer to the surface in semiarid and arid climates where precipitation is scarce. Capillary action brings cations like calcium and sodium dissolved in soil water upwards where they precipitate from the water.

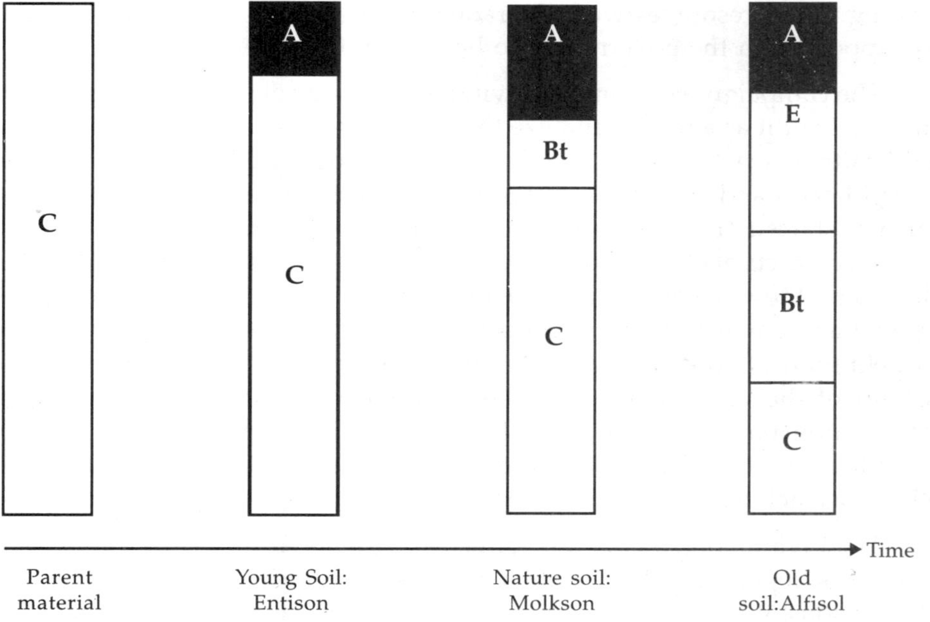

Fig. 2.1: Eluviation and illuviation under humid, semiarid and arid conditions

C Horizon

The C horizon represents the soil parent material, either created in situ or transported into its present location. Beneath the C horizon lies bedrock.

The preceding paragraphs describe a generic soil profile, yet not all soils have each one of the horizons, nor are they all the same with respect to thickness composition and structure. Newly formed "immature" soils may only have an O-A-C sequence while older more "mature" soils display the full profile of horizons as described earlier. The particular compositional, structural and chemical composition of the soil depends on the various factors that influence soil formation.

EFFECT OF FERTILIZERS

Indiscriminate use of chemical fertilizers over several decades has been sucking life out of Indian soils, and thereby putting the country's food security at stake. But the government has continued to mindlessly promote chemical fertilizers through their lenient subsidy policy.

It was under those circumstances that Greenpeace India decided to set out on a journey, seven months ago, to listen to what the real stakeholders – the farmers – have to say about the issue. Surprisingly, we found that they were equally worried and caught in a vicious cycle of chemical intensive farming. Their resources were degraded, their fortunes lost, and there was no support from the government to help them tide over the crisis.

The campaign was named "Living Soils", and soil conservationist used the social audit as a tool to analyze the impact of the government policies on soil health. It was probably the first time ever social audits were conducted on soil health and support systems in India or elsewhere in the world. The journey started from Assam, a north eastern state in India and covered selected districts of Orissa, Karnataka, Madhya Pradesh and Punjab. Wherever they went, the villagers championed the cause. They were at the fore front, organizing demonstrations, street plays and public hearings. It proved to be a celebration of soils. It was quite evident that farmers were desperate to get out of the vicious cycle and keen to adopt an alternative, ecological fertilization pathway. Not only, farmers but also other stakeholders of agriculture, who participated in the public hearings, voiced the same views. What was lacking was support from the government.

The Living Soils report was launched by a noted film Director, Anusha Rizvi. The report, titled, "Of Soils, Subsidies and Survival", captured the observations, views and aspirations of the farmers and puts them alongside the scientific literature available on the topic. Interestingly, there is a very positive response from the Finance Ministry. The main recommendation in the report, creation of a National Ecological Fertilization Mission, as a first step to shift subsidies from chemical fertilizers to ecological fertilization is well received.

In engineering, soil is referred to as regolith, or loose rock material. Soil is a natural body consisting of layers of mineral constituents of variable thicknesses, which differ from the parent materials in their morphological, physical, chemical, and mineralogical characteristics.

COMPOSITION OF SOIL

Soil is composed of particles of broken rock that have been altered by chemical and environmental processes that include weathering and erosion. Soil differs from its parent rock due to interactions between the lithosphere, hydrosphere, atmosphere, and the biosphere. It is a mixture of mineral and organic constituents that are in solid, gaseous and aqueous states. Soil is commonly referred to as dirt.

Soil particles pack loosely, forming a soil structure filled with pore spaces. These pores contain soil solution (liquid) and air (gas). Accordingly, soils are often treated as a three state system. Most soils have a density between 1 and 2 g/cm^3. Soil is also known as earth: it is the substance from which our planet takes its name. Little of the soil composition of planet Earth is older than the Tertiary and most no older than the Pleistocene.

SOIL FORMATION AND DEVELOPMENT

Soil formation is the combined effect of physical, chemical, biological, and anthropogenic processes on soil parent material. It is also called 'pedogenesis'. Soil genesis involves processes that develop layers or horizons in the soil profile. These processes involve additions, losses, transformations and translocations of material that compose the soil. Minerals derived from weathered rocks undergo changes that cause the formation of secondary minerals and other compounds that are variably soluble in water, these constituents are moved (translocated) from one area of the soil to other areas by water and animal activity. The alteration and movement of materials within soil causes the formation of distinctive soil horizons.

Weathering is the first stage in the transforming of parent material into soil material. In soils forming from bedrock, a thick layer of weathered material called saprolite may form. Saprolite is the result of weathering processes that include: hydrolysis (the replacement of a mineral's cations with hydrogen ions), chelation from organic compounds, hydration (the absorption of water by minerals), solution of minerals by water, and physical processes that include freezing and thawing or wetting and drying.The mineralogical and chemical composition of the primary bedrock material, plus physical features, including grain size and degree of consolidation, plus the rate and type of weathering, transforms it into different soil materials.

The weathering of bedrock produces the parent material from which soils form. An example of soil development from bare rock occurs on recent lava flows in warm regions under heavy and very frequent rainfall. In such climates, plants become established very quickly on basaltic lava, even though there is very little organic material. The plants are supported by the porous rock as it is filled with nutrient-bearing water which carries, for example, dissolved minerals and guano. The developing plant roots, themselves or associated with my corrhizal fungi, gradually break up the porous lava and organic matter soon accumulates.

But even before it does, the predominantly porous broken lava in which the plant roots grow can be considered a soil. How the soil "life" cycle proceeds is influenced by at least five classic soil forming factors that are dynamically intertwined in shaping the way soil is developed, they include: parent material, regional climate, topography, biotic potential and the passage of time.

The material from which soil forms is called parent material. It includes: weathered primary bedrock; secondary material transported from other locations, e.g. colluvium and alluvium; deposits that are already present but mixed or altered in other ways - old soil formations, organic material including peator alpine humus; and anthropogenic materials, like landfill or mine waste. Few soils form directly from the breakdown of the underlying rocks they develop on.

Residual Soils

These soils are often called "residual soils", and have the same general chemistry as their parent rocks. Most soils derive from materials that have been transported from other locations by wind, water and gravity. Some of these materials may have moved many miles or only a few feet. Windblown material called loess is common in the Midwest of North America and in Central Asia and other locations. Glacial till is a component of many soils in the northern and southern latitudes and those formed near large mountains; till is the product of glacial ice moving over the ground. The ice can break rock and larger stones into smaller pieces, it also can sort material into different sizes. As glacial ice melts, the melt water also moves and sorts material, and deposits it varying distances from its origin. The deeper sections of the soil profile may have materials that are relatively unchanged from when they were deposited by water, ice or wind.

Climate

Soil formation greatly depends on the climate, and soils from different climate zones show distinctive charac-teristics. Temperature and moisture affect weathering and leaching. Wind moves sand and other particles, especially in arid regions where there is little plant cover. The type and amount of precipitation influence soil formation by affecting the movement of ions and particles through the soil, aiding in the development of different soil profiles. Seasonal and daily temperature fluctuations affect the effectiveness of water in weathering parent rock material and affect soil dynamics. The cycle of freezing and thawing is an effective mechanism to break up rocks and other consolidated materials. Temperature and precipitation rates affect biological activity, rates of chemical reactions and types of vegetation cover.

Biological Factors

Plants, animals, fungi, bacteria and humans affect soil formation. Animals and micro-organisms mix soils to form burrows and pores allowing moisture and gases to seep into deeper layers. In the same way, plant roots open channels in the soils, especially plants with deep taproots which can penetrate many meters through the different soil layers to bring up nutrients from deeper in the soil. Plants with fibrous roots that spread out near the soil surface, have roots that are easily decomposed, adding organic matter. Micro-organisms, including fungi and bacteria, affect chemical exchanges between roots and soil and act as a reserve of nutrients. Humans can impact soil formation by removing vegetation cover; this removal promotes erosion. They can also mix the different soil layers, restarting the soil formation process as less-weathered material is mixed with and diluting the more developed upper layers. Some soils may contain up to one million species of microbes per gram, most of those species being unknown, making soil the most abundant ecosystem on Earth.

Vegetation impacts soils in numerous ways. It can prevent erosion caused by the impact of rain or surface runoff. Plants shade soils, keeping them cooler and slowing evaporation of soil moisture, or plants by way of transpiration can cause soils to lose moisture. Plants can form new chemicals which can break down or build up soil particles. The type and amount of vegetation depends on climate, land form topography, soil characteristics, and biological factors. Soil factors such as density, depth, chemistry, pH, temperature and moisture greatly affect the type of plants that can grow in a given location. Dead plants and dropped leaves and stems fall to the surface of the soil and decompose. There, organisms feed on them and mix the organic material with the upper soil layers; these added organic compounds become part of the soil formation process.

Everchanging Soil

Soil is always changing.It takes about 800 to 1000 years for a 2.5 cm thick layer of fertile soil to be formed in nature. Time is a factor in the interactions of all the above factors as they develop soil. Over time, soils evolve features dependent on the other forming factors, and soil formation is a time-responsive process dependent on how the other factors interplay with each other. For example, recently-deposited material from a flood exhibits no soil development because there has not been enough time for soil-forming activities. The soil surface is buried, and the formation process begins again for this soil. The long periods over which change occurs and its multiple influences mean that simple soils are rare, resulting in the formation of soil horizons. While soil can achieve relative stability in properties for extended periods, the soil life cycle ultimately ends in soil conditions that leave it vulnerable to erosion. Despite the inevitability of soil retrogression and degradation, most soil cycles are long and productive.

Soil-forming factors continue to affect soils during their existence, even on "stable" landscapes that are long-enduring, some for millions of years. Materials are deposited on top and materials are blown or washed away from the surface. With additions, removals and alterations, soils are always subject to new conditions. Whether these are slow or rapid changes depend on climate, landscape position and biological activity.

Formation of Rocks

Rocks are the chief sources for the parent materials over which soils are developed. There are three main kinds of rocks:

1. igneous rocks;
2. sedimentary rocks; and
3. metamorphic rocks.

Igneous Rocks

They are formed by the cooling, hardening and crystallizing of various kinds of lavas and differ widely in their chemical composition. They chiefly contain feldspars, maphic minerals and quartz. Rocks containing a high proportion of quartz (60-75%) are classified as acidic, whereas those containing less than 50% quartz are classified as basic. The common igneous rocks found in India are the granites(acidic) and basalts or the Deccan Trap (basic)

Sedimentary Rocks

They are derived from igneous rocks and are formed by the consolidation of fragmentary rock materials and the products of their decomposition deposited by water. The common sedimentary rocks are conglo-merate, sandstone, shale and limestone. Alluvial, glacial and aeolian deposits form the unconsolidated sedimentary rocks.

Metamorphic Rocks

They are formed from the igneous or sedimentary rocks by the action of intense heat and high pressure or both resulting in considerable change in the texture and mineral composition. The common meta-morphic rocks are gneis from granite, quartzite from quartz or sandstone, marble from limestone and slate from shale.

The rocks vary greatly in chemical composition. Table 2.1 gives the average composition of four different kinds of rocks.

Table 2.1: Percentage Chemical Composition of Rocks

Oxides	Igneous Rocks	Shales	Sandstones	Limestones
SiO_2	59.07	58.90	78.64	5.20
Al_2O_3	15.22	15.63	4.77	0.81
Fe_2O_3	3.10	4.07	1.08	0.54
MgO	3.45	2.47	1.17	7.92
FeO	3.71	2.48	0.32	...
CaO	5.10	3.15	5.51	42.74
Na_2O	3.71	1.32	0.45	0.05
K_2O	3.11	3.28	1.32	0.33
O_2	...	2.67	5.03	41.70
P_2O_5	0.30	0.17	.08	0.04
MnO	0.11	...	...	...
TiO_3	1.03	0.66	0.25	0.06
H_2O	1.30	3.72	1.33	0.56
Miscellaneous	0.79	1.48	0.07	0.05

Weathering refers to the physical and chemical disintegration and decomposition of rocks which are not under equilibrium under temperature, pressure and moisture conditions on the earth's surface. In the beginning, weathering precedes soil formation, more so in hard rocks. In other words, weatheringcreates the parent material over which soil formation takes place. Later, weathering, soil formation and development proceed simultaneously. The weathering may be physical or chemical.

INDIAN SOILS

The soils in India are when rocks break down into very small pieces by natural forces. Alluvial, black, red, laterite, mountain and desert are different types of soils. Removal of minerals from the soil due to passing of water through it is called 'leaching'.

Fertilizer formed from dead leaves and plants in the soil. Which is called humus. Located in southern Asia between Myanmar and Pakistan, India has 1,147,956 square miles of land. Its terrain varies from the upland plain (Deccan Plateau) in the south, to flat to rolling plains along the Ganga River, with deserts in the west and the Himalaya Mountains in the north, according to the CIA World Factbook. Rocks weathered over time and decaying matter form soil, the loose material that is the topmost layer of the Earth's surface. The amounts present of three basic textures—clay, sand and silt—help determine India's eight major soil types.

Alluvial Soils

Alluvial soils come from the silt that washes down into rivers. Found by rivers and nearby areas that flood, "alluvium consists of silt, sand, clay, and gravel and often contains a good deal of organic matter," according to the Encyclopaedia Britannica.

This fertile soil ranges from tan and coarse textured in the upper sections of rivers to dark and very fine textured in the delta areas. India's farmers grow cotton, jute, rice, sugarcane and wheat in alluvial soil, which is rich in potash and humus, but with a low phosphorous and nitrogen content.

Vertisols or Black Soils

Vertisols, or black soils, have high clay content, and a high ability to retain moisture. Vertisols range from dark grey to black and develop cracks in the summer. Unlike alluvial soils, black soils lack organic matter, but like alluvial soils, Vertisols have low amounts of phosphorous and nitrogen. However, Vertisols have a great deal of iron, lime, calcium, alumina, carbonates and magnesium. Farmers grow cotton, groundnut, millets, oilseeds, rice and wheat in Vertisols.

Red Soils

Red soils are more sand than clay and do not retain moisture. Red soils form from the weathering of old crystalline rocks and this soil is slightly acidic. Like alluvium and Vertisols, red soils are poor in phosphorous and nitrogen. Red soils are also low in lime but have iron and a small amount of humus. Farmers grow groundnut, millet, potatoes, rice, sugarcane tobacco and wheat in red soils.

Laterite Soils

These are formed when temperatures are high and there are wet and dry periods with high rainfall during the wet periods that leaches silica, but leaves iron and aluminum oxides behind, which is known as Laterite, according to WiZiQ. When exposed to air the brown to yellowish soil becomes hard, making it a good building material. Cashew, coconut, coffee, rubber and tea trees grow in the soil, which is rich in iron and poor in lime, magnesium and potash.

Desert Soils

These are porous and coarse being 90 per cent sand and five per cent clay, with a low moisture content. This soil comes from weathering and wind deposit. This soil is rich in nitrates and phosphates but lacks nitrogen. Drought resistant crops such as barley and millet grow in desert soil.

Mountain Soils

These soils range from sandy to loamy in texture and are formed from organic matter from forests deposited in the slopes of hills. Farmers grow coffee, spices, tea and tropical fruits in it.

Saline and Alkaline Soils

These soils are also sandy to loamy in texture but they contain salts, like calcium, magnesium and sodium and this infertile soil type is not suitable for agriculture.

Peaty and Marshy Soils

These soils were formed by an accumulation of organic material in humid areas, but this black soil is very acidic and heavy. Peat bogs and marshes are not used for agriculture.

Characteristics

Soil colour is often the first impression one has when viewing soil. Striking colours and contrasting patterns are especially memorable. The Red River (Mississippi watershed) carries sediment eroded from extensive reddish soils like Port Silt Loam in Oklahoma. The Yellow River in China carries yellow sediment from eroding loessal soils.Mollisols in the Great Plains are darkened and enriched by organic matter. Podsols inboreal forests have highly contrasting layers due to acidity and leaching. Soil colour is primarily influenced by soil mineralogy. Many soil colours are due to the extensive and various iron minerals.

The development and distribution of colour in a soil profile result from chemical and biological weathering, especially redox reactions. As the primary minerals in soil parent material weather, the elements combine into new and colourful compounds. Iron forms secondary minerals with a yellow or red colour, organic matter decomposes into black and brown compounds, and manganese, sulfur and nitrogen can form black mineral deposits.

These pigments produce various colour patterns due to effects by the environment during soil formation. Aerobic conditions produce uniform or gradual colour changes, while reducing environments result in disrupted colour flow with complex, mottled patterns and points of colour concentration.

What is Soil Structure?

Soil structure is the arrangement of soil particles into aggregates. These may have various shapes, sizes and degrees of development or expression. Soil structure affects aeration, water movement, resistance to erosion and plant root growth. Structure often gives clues to texture, organic matter content, biological activity, past soil evolution, human use, and chemical and mineralogical conditions under which the soil formed. If the soil is too high in clay, adding gypsum, washed river sand and organic matter will balance the composition. Adding organic matter to soil that is depleted in nutrients and too high in sand will boost the quality.

Soil texture refers to sand, silt and clay composition. Soil content affects soil behaviour, including the retention capacity for nutrients and water. Sand and silt are the products of physical weathering, while clay is the product of chemical weathering. Clay content has retention capacity for nutrients and water. Clay soils resist wind and water erosion better than silty and sandy soils, because the particles are more tightly joined to each other. In medium-textured soils, clay is often translocated downward through the soil profile and accumulates in the subsoil.

Soil resistivity is a measure of a soil's ability to retard the conduction of an electric current. The electrical resistivity of soil can affect the rate of galvanic corrosion of metallic structures in contact with the soil. Higher moisture content or increased electrolyte concentration can lower the resistivity and increase the conductivity thereby increasing the rate of corrosion. Soil resistivity values typically range from about 2 to 1000 Ù·m, but more extreme values are not unusual.

SOIL HORIZONS

It is based on the type of material the horizons are composed of; these materials reflect the duration of the specific processes used in soil formation. They are labeled using a short hand notation of letters and numbers. They are described and classified by their colour, size, texture, structure, consistency, root quantity, pH, voids, boundary characteristics, and if they have nodules or concretions. Any one soil profile does not have all the major horizons covered below; soils may have few or many horizons.

The exposure of parent material to favourable conditions produces initial soils that are suitable for plant growth. Plant growth often results in the accumulation of organic residues, the accumulated organic layer is called the O horizon. Biological organisms colonize and break down organic materials, making available nutrients that other plants and animals can live on. After sufficient time a distinctive organic surface layer forms with humus which is called the A horizon.

Classification

Soil is classified into categories in order to understand relationships between different soils and to determine the usefulness of a soil for a particular use. One of the first classification systems was developed by the Russian scientist Dokuchaev around 1880. It was modified a number of times by American and European researchers, and developed into the system commonly used until the 1960s. It was based on the idea that soils have a particular morphology based on the materials and factors that form them. In the 1960s, a different classification system began to emerge, that focused on soil morphology instead of parental materials and soil-forming factors. Since then it has undergone further modifications. The World Reference Base for Soil Resources (WRB) aims to establish an international reference base for soil classification.

Soil Taxonomy

In the United States, soil orders are the highest hierarchical level of soil classification in the USDA Soil Taxonomy classification system. Names of the orders end with the suffix-sol. There are 12 soil orders in Soil Taxonomy:

- *Entisol* - recently formed soils that lack well-developed horizons. Commonly found on unconsolidated sediments like sand, some have an A horizon on top of bedrock.
- *Vertisol* - inverted soils. They tend to swell when wet and shrink upon drying, often forming deep cracks that surface layers can fall into.
- *Inceptisol* - young soils. They have subsurface horizon formation but show little eluviation and illuviation.
- *Aridisol* - dry soils forming under desert conditions. They include nearly 20 per cent of soils on Earth. Soil formation is slow, and accumulated organic matter is scarce. They may have subsurface zones (calcic horizons) where calcium carbonates have accumulated from percolating water. Many aridiso soils have well-developed Bt horizons showing clay movement from past periods of greater moisture.

- *Mollisol* - soft soils with very thick A horizons.
- *Spodosol* - soils produced by podsolization. They are typical soils of coniferous and deciduous forests in cooler climates.
- *Alfisol* - soils with aluminium and iron. They have horizons of clay accumulation, and form where there is enough moisture and warmth for at least three months of plant growth.
- *Ultisol* - soils that are heavily leached.
- *Oxisol* - soil with heavy oxide content.
- *Histosol* - organic soils.
- *Andisols* - volcanic soils, which tend to be high in glass content.
- *Gelisols* - permafrost soils.

Most living things in soils, including plants, insects, bacteria and fungi, are dependent on organic matter for nutrients and energy. Soils often have varying degrees of organic compounds in different states of decomposition. Many soils, including desert and rocky-gravel soils, have no or little organic matter. Soils that are all organic matter, such as peat (histosols), are infertile.

Defining Humus

It refers to organic matter that has decomposed to a point where it is resistant to further breakdown or alteration. Humic acids and fulvic acids are important constituents of humus and typically form from plant residues like foliage, stems and roots. After death, these plant residues begin to decay, starting the formation of humus. Humus formation involves changes within the soil and plant residue, there is a reduction of water soluble constituents including cellulose and hemicellulose; as the residues are deposited and break down, humin, lignin and lignin complexes accumulate within the soil; as micro-organisms live and feed on the decaying plant matter, an increase in proteins occurs.

Lignin is resistant to breakdown and accumulates within the soil; it also chemically reacts with amino acids which add to its resistance to decomposition, including enzymatic decomposition by microbes Fats and axes from plant atter have some resistance to decomposition and persist in soils for a while.

Clay soils often have higher organic contents that persist longer than soils without clay. Proteins normally decompose readily, but when bound to clay particles they become more resistant to decomposition.

Clay particles also absorb enzymes that would break down proteins. The addition of organic matter to clay soils can render the organic matter and any added nutrients inaccessible to plants and microbes for many years, since they can bind strongly to the clay. High soil tannin (polyphenol) content from plants can cause nitrogen to be sequestered by proteins or cause nitrogen immobilization, also making nitrogen unavailable to plants.

Humus formation is a process dependent on the amount of plant material added each year and the type of base soil; both are affected by climate and the type of organisms present. Soils with humus can vary in nitrogen content but have 3 to 6 per cent nitrogen typically; humus, as a reserve of nitrogen and phosphorus, is a vital component affecting soil fertility. Humus also absorbs water, acting as a moisture reserve, that plants can utilize; it also expands and shrinks between dry and wet states, providing pore spaces. Humus is less stable than other soil constituents, because it is affected by microbial decomposition, and over time its concentration decreases without the addition of new organic matter. However, some forms of humus are highly stable and may persist over centuries if not millennia: they are issued from the slow oxidation of charcoal, also called black carbon, like in Amazonian Terra preta or Black Earths, or from the sequestration of humic compounds within mineral horizons, like in podzols.

Retaining Water

Soils retain water that can dissolve a range of molecules and ions. These solutions exchange gases with the soil atmosphere, contain dissolved sugars, fulvic acids and other organic acids, plant nutrients such as nitrate, ammonium, potassium, phosphate, sulfate and calcium, and micronutrients such as zinc, iron and copper. These nutrients are exchanged with the mineral and humic component, that retains them in its ionic state, by adsorption. Some arid soils have sodium solutions that greatly impact plant growth. Soil pH can affect the type and amount of anions and cations that soil solutions contain and that exchange with the soil substrate and biological organisms.

Study of Biogeography

Biogeography is the study of special variations in biological communities. Soils are a restricting factor as to which plants can grow in which environments. Soil scientists survey soils in the hope of understanding controls as to what vegetation can and will grow in a particular location.

Geologists also have a particular interest in the patterns of soil on the surface of the earth. Soil texture, colour and chemistry often reflect the underlying geologic parent material, and soil types often change at geologic unit boundaries. Buried paleosols mark previous land surfaces and record climatic conditions from previous eras. Geologists use this paleopedological record to understand the ecological relationships in past ecosystems.

According to the theory of biorhexistasy, prolonged conditions conducive to forming deep, weathered soils result in increasing ocean salinity and the formation of limestone.

Geologists use soil profile features to establish the duration of surface stability in the context ofgeologic faults or slope stability. An offset subsoil horizon indicates rupture during soil formation and the degree of subsequent subsoil formation is relied upon to establish time since rupture.

Soil examined in shovel test pits is used by archaeologists for relative dating based on stratigraphy (as opposed to absolute dating). What is considered most typical is to use soil profile features to determine the maximum reasonable pit depth than needs to be examined for archaeological evidence in the interest ofcultural resources management.

Soils altered or formed by humans (anthropic and anthropogenic soils) are also of interest to archaeologists, such as terra preta soils.

3 Land Drainage Practice

Drains are constructed and are pre-requisite for carrying excess water off agricultural land. Without drains to remove water, the soil becomes waterlogged hampering the growth of crops and pasture. Drainage is essential in establishing good productive land. There are multiple types of drainage systems. Before designing the drainage system, it is important to consider what will be appropriate for your needs and where the drain is carrying the water to.

Proper planning, design, construction and maintenance of both surface and subsurface drains and channels will minimise the likelihood that they will cause environmental harm and alleviate some of their adverse effects. It is preferable to drain in the dry months to minimise muddying of downstream waterways. This will also increase the chance that the drains can be revegetated before water starts running again.

Drain Planning

Careful planning should be undertaken when planning drainage.

Prior to drain planning, it is important to consider these points :

- Ensure the land can be drained.
- Determine whether the soil types are able to sustain drainage.
- Check the possibility of acid sulfate soils or salinity occurring.
- Know where the drains will move water to. Will this impact on the downstream environment?

- Know the land capabilities. Will the natural slope of the land sustain drainage? If so, can the drain be changed or modified to suit the application?
- Gain knowledge of the likely flood events or extent of waterlogging. Will your drain have the capacity to pass the size of the flood or amount of water concerned? Find out about Floodplain Mapping for your area.
- Don't over-design the drain.
- Seek appropriate advice according to the prevailing circumstances. This may, in many circumstances, only require some levels to be taken. For larger drainage systems, in-depth soil analysis and design engineering might be required.

EFFECTIVE DRAIN MANAGEMENT

Caring for drains is similar to caring for streams. Activities that occur in the catchments affect the stream once water discharges from the catchment. Effective drain management is important for preventing environmental problems. Sediments, nutrients (fertilisers), herbicides, pesticides, organic wastes or pollutants washed into the drains flow into the stream and impact on water quality downstream.

Grass cover or other effective plant coverage of the drain should be encouraged to prevent eroding soil moving into the waterway. Grass assists in holding the banks together. When constructing the drain, it is important to analyse the soil type, as some soils are more prone to erosion than others. Steep, severe drain banks (batters) should be avoided in most situations. Banks at too steep an angle (batters) are more likely to erode than gentle gradients.

Runoff Speed and Erosion

Drains constructed in sloping country also have the potential to increase water velocity, thus an increase in energy is produced. Energy is caused by increasing the "speed" of the water flow and this has the potential to cause erosive affects, where "head cutting" (gouging out of the bottom and sides of the drain) and drain bank erosion can occur, resulting in sediment transportation and downstream siltation. There is a tendency among those wishing to drain land to remove floodwaters as quickly as possible from the flood prone areas.

Sometimes the "slowing down" of water being drained from an area is one of the most useful and effective methods of minimising the above-mentioned erosive affects. There are several methods that can be considered and applied, such as:

- Retaining areas of bushland, particularly alongside drains, to slow runoff.
- Increase the drain length by not straightening existing waterways, drains or creeks. This reduces the steepness of the drainage system and stops water running off too quickly, thus minimising erosion.
- Construct paddock drains to achieve effective drainage, but on minimal gradients where possible.
- Installation of the smallest but most effective possible outlets from drainage zones. This has the effect of reducing sediment and nutrient transp-ortation by allowing a lesser discharge of water. This method is often used in the Hump and Hollow drainage application, but can be used with the more conventional open ditch applications.
- Installation of simple rock riffles and drop structures. These can be placed in areas where erosion has or is likely to occur. Advice on these structures, particularly for larger applications, should be sought from technical experts. Engineers such as Department of Primary Industries, Water and Environment River Engineering staff and Regional Water Management Officers are a good first point of contact.

Purpose

The purpose of the drain must be ascertained so excess water can be moved without damaging the downstream environment. It is possible that removing a flooding problem by building a drainage system in an upstream area could cause, or add to, the severity of flooding downstream. This means the flooding problem has not been rectified, only moved.

Stock

Stock access to the drains should also be controlled, just as stock access to riparian land needs to be managed, to prevent stream bank damage. Fencing drains prevents stock from damaging and depositing organic matter into the drain, and subsequently the catchment. This has the benefit of cutting down on maintenance costs associated with desilting the drain.

Planning of Weeds Control

Weed control methods should be undertaken as a yearly event and should be carefully planned. Failure to do so could result in drains becoming ineffective, and selection of the wrong methods for weed control can be an expensive mistake. If using chemical sprays, selection of the correct chemicals is critical to ensure effective weed control and is critical to ensure animals living in the drain are not killed. Some drains sustain life such as frogs and fish, some of which may be threatened species.

Controlling Weed Growth

There is a need to control weed growth, other foliage growth and siltation in drains to maximise the effectiveness of the drainage system and to reduce further weed spread and flooding occurring. Drains must be regularly inspected and maintained to achieve long-term effectiveness in performance for removing water. A typical maintenance programme should includes:

- spraying.
- removal of weeds.
- reduction of nutrient sources (that some weeds thrive on!).
- reduction of sunlight by retaining tree growth alongside drains thus minimising weed infestations.
- inspection to see if stock have broken, and gone through, fences thus damaging drains.

Land drainage can be distinguished in surface and subsurface drainage.

Principle of Surface Drainage

Surface drainage deals in principle with water-logging on the land surface and subsurface drainage deals in principle with water-logging in the soil, i.e. the water table is too shallow for the purpose the land is used. Interaction between the two kinds of drainage may occur: surface drainage may reduce the need of subsurface drainage and *vice versa*. To accomplish the drainage function one needs drainage systems, which can be discerned into field and main drainage systems.

Field drainage systems do the actual work of water-logging control while main drainage systems are designed to collect the water from the field drainage systems and transport it to the outlet. The outlet may work by gravity or it may be equipped with a pumping station. Some outlets are designed too work part time by gravity and part time by pumping. Pumping stations may also be found in the interior along main drains. When subsurface drainage is accomplished by wells, these also need a water lifting device.

Field drainage systems can be regular or checked systems. Regular systems work immediately when waterlogging threatens to occur as a result of a considerable recharge, e.g. rainfall, irrigation.Checked systems are systems designed to operate only occasionally.

Examples of application of checked systems can be found in rice growing areas where drainage is normally not required except during certain periods, e.g. during harvest, during exceptionally intensive rainstorms, or to allow the land to dry between crops.

Another example is the closure of drains or the reduction of the drainage capacity during dry spells to conserve water and reduce the losses. Subsurface drainage by wells and pumps constitute automatically checked systems because there is always the possibility to switch off the pumps.

Surface field drainage systems are usually made by land forming/ shaping. The regular systems consist of graded land or bedded land using shallow open drains to collect the water. Checked systems consist of bunded basins (in flat land) or bunded terraces (in sloping land). Bunded terraces in sloping land are more often used for erosion control and water conservation than for drainage, yet these sloping lands may occasionally need surface drainage. Regular subsurface field drainage can be done using subsurface drains viz. mole drains, ditches, tile drains, pipe drains or subsoiling (deep plowing). Mole drains and deep plowing can only be practiced in clay soils. It is a common misunderstanding that a ditch drain invariably would be a surface drain. Although shallow ditches are used in surface drainage to collect and transport water and may be called surface drains, the deeper ditches can have an important function in the control of the water table and thus are subsurface drains by the definition given above.

In fact, subsurface drainage by ditches is more effective than by pipe drains, but sometimes the open ditches may be a hindrance and the maintenance may be a nuisance. Checked subsurface drainage systems consist of ditches and pipe drains equipped with check structures or pumped outlets as well as of pumped wells.

Drainage Water for Irrigation

If the water quality permits, drainage water can be reused for irrigation. Especially deep wells are useful for this purpose. Thus the water-table may be lowered by pumping during dry spells while an extra underground storage facility is created to be filled up during wet spells. During wet spells it may be desirable to halt or reduce the pumping from wells as no immediate irrigation water is required and the extra storage capacity created in the underground during dry spells now comes in handy.

In irrigated lands of the (semi)arid regions, the drainage water also carries salts and helps to maintain a favorablesalt balance in the soil. All irrigation water, however "sweet", bring salts that remain behind in the soil after evaporation. For example, assuming irrigation water with a low salt concentration of 0.3 g/l (equal to 0.3 kg/m^3 corresponding to an electric conductivity of about 0.5 dS/m) and a modest annual supply of irrigation water of 10000 m^3/ha (barely 3 mm/day) already brings 3000 kg salt/ha each year. In the absence of sufficient natural drainage (as in waterlogged soils) and without a proper leaching and drainage programme, this would lead in the long run to a highsoil salinity that may need to be checked by salinity control.

DRAINAGE IN AGRICULTURAL FIELDS

Principles

Land drainage is principally used to alleviate waterlogging in agricultural fields, but it can also dessiccate certain ground types in prolonged dry spells, so think carefully before installing. Note that land drainage is not the same as a soakaway, although they may both be used to dispose of surface and/or groundwater.

Other uses for land drainage are as dispersal drains for septic systems and as collector drains where more formal drainage fittings would be inappropriate. It is also an essential part of civil engineering projects, where the use of fin drains and drainage composites is gradually replacing the more traditional forms of land drainage.

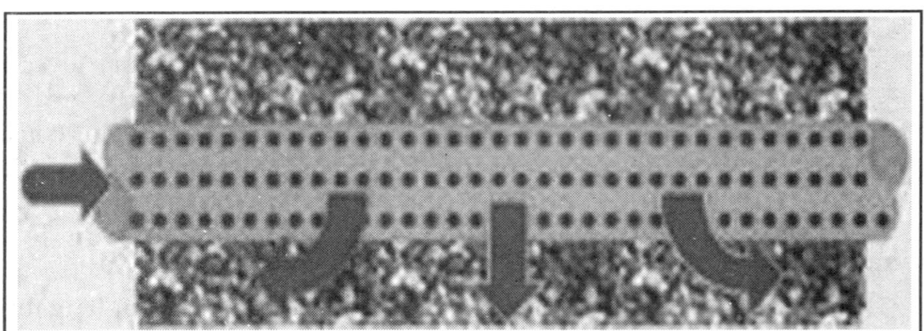

Fig. 3.1: Dispersal Drain - returns water to the ground

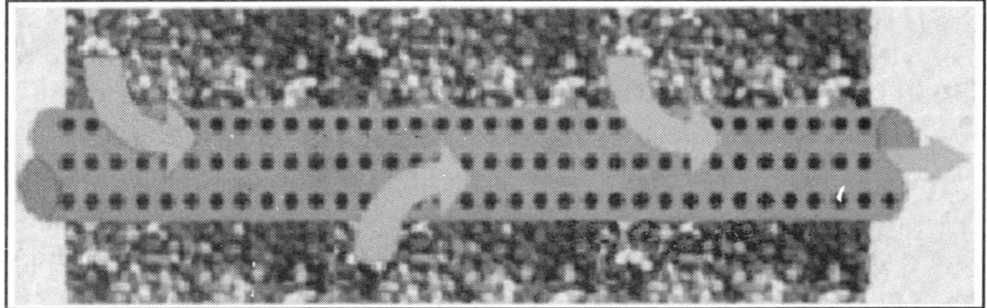

Fig. 3.2: Collector Drain - removes water from the ground

Land drainage works by providing an open conduit for groundwater to follow to a disposal point, or, in the case of dispersal drains, to a dispersal area or leach field. There are a few variations on this theme, involving the type of backfill material, and the type of pre-formed conduit that is used, but all rely on two simple principles; that the land drain provides a 'path of least resistance' for groundwater to follow, and that, left to its own devices, water flows down even the gentlest of slopes.

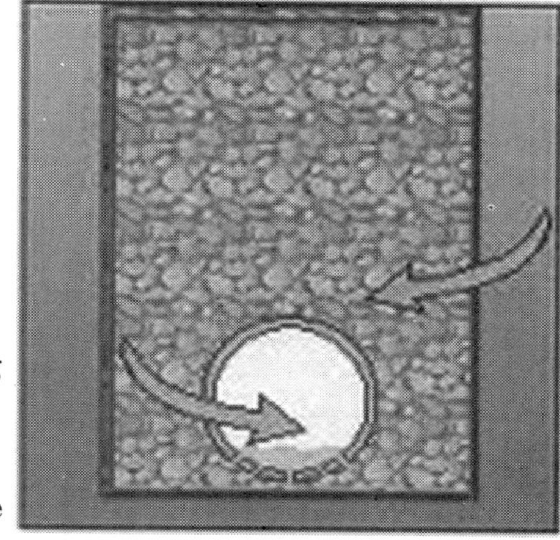

Fig. 3.3: The flow of groundwater in a typical land drain

Groundwater is held by soils within pores, which are the small voids or interstices between the grains that make up the soil. The bedding material surrounding a land drain has significantly larger pores between each stone, providing more space for the groundwater to occupy. The centre of the pipe itself can be thought of as one big pore. Therefore, in a collector drain, there is a 'gradient' of hydrostatic pressure from the soil, via the bedding into the pipe, along which the groundwater will migrate to the point of lowest hydrostatic pressure, ie, the inside of the pipe.

In a dispersal drain, the gradient is reversed because water is being continually added to the pipe from the septic tank or other source, and so the hydrostatic pressure is greatest inside the pipe, causing the flow to be from pipe to soil, rather than from soil to pipe.

Soil mechanics and hydro-dynamics is a major field within the discipline of civil engineering and is far beyond the remit of this site, but, hopefully, this will have given some insight into the basic principles involved in ground water management.

The disposal point of a land drain system, whether it's a manhole, a soakaway, a leach field or an outfall, is always at the lowest point of the system.

Try as we might, we haven't yet managed to get water to flow uphill. During the summer, land drainage can sometimes be identified by lusher growth of vegetation over the line of drainage, and this phenomenon is even more pronounced in situations where land drainage has been used to disperse the processed effluent of a septic tank. This could be turned to your garden's advantage with a little pre-planning.

Why We Need Outfall

Land drainage, whether it has been installed in order to drain an area of soggy ground, or to disperse water collected from hard surfaces or the effluent from a septic tank, must have an outfall, ie, a point where it can 'empty' itself.

Filter and collector systems (Fig. 3.4) often discharge, or "outfall", into a ditch or stream, but they can be connected to the surface water system of a property if there is absolutely no possible alternative, or if your local water board do not permit outfalls to natural watercourses.

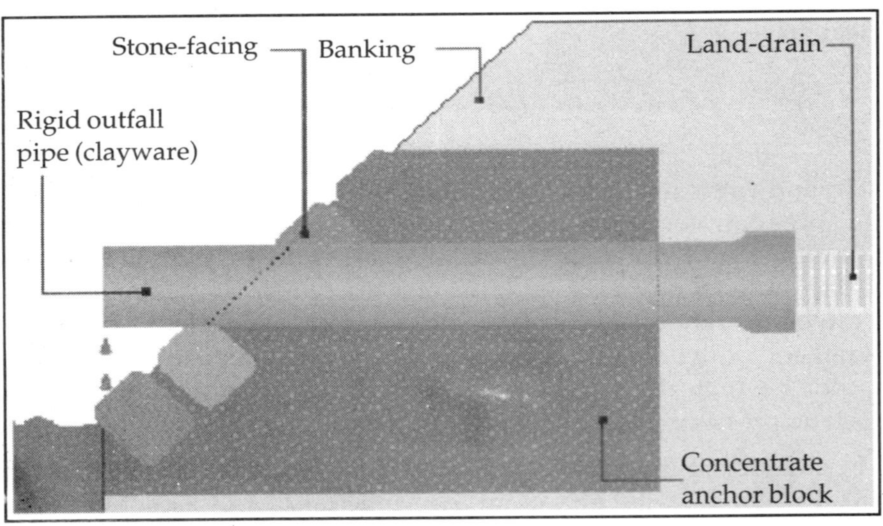

Fig. 3.4: Outfall cross-section detail

Only in the most exceptional of circumstances should land drainage be outfalled to a combined or a foul water system, and, if it is, the connection must be via a trap to prevent smells, effluent and/or raw sewage entering the land drainage system.

For outfalling to a ditch or other watercourse (assuming there is no problem with consent from the land-owner or water authority), the outfall pipe, preferably clay or rigid plastic, needs to be anchored into the bank with a large block of concrete. It's essential that the section of bank directly beneath the outfall pipe is adequately protected from erosion by means of a stone or concrete apron.

Most local authorities and/or water boards have their own specification for an outfall detail, but the illustration opposite shows the the type of scheme favoured by many authorities for small outfalls. Larger outfalls, such as those serving an extensive land-drainage or surface water system, those discharging into a fast-flowing watercourse or those with pipes of diameter greater than 225 mm, may involve cast in-situ concrete structures and possibly steel piling driven into the river-bed. In all cases, consult your local authority before commencing work.

Catch Pits

On filter/collector land drainage systems that have not used a geo-textile to minimise soil particle or sediment migration, a catch-pit should be considered preceding any outfall to a natural watercourse, to remove grits, silts and excess sediment. A catch-pit is, essentially, an empty chamber with an inlet pipe and an outlet pipe set at a level above the floor of the pit. Any sediment carried by the system settles out whilst in the catch pit, from where it can be periodically pumped out or removed.

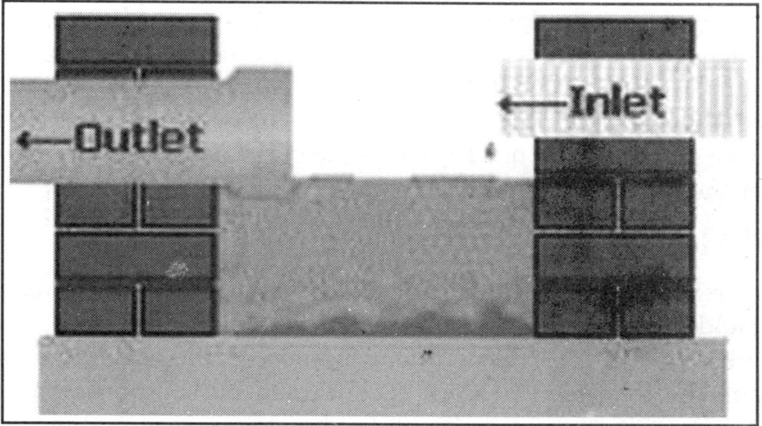

Fig. 3.5: A typical site-constructed catch pit

Herringbone Pattern

Where land drainage is used to drain a larger garden, it should be installed in the classic herringbone pattern to ensure no point within the area is more than 2.5 m from a drain. Some pre-planning is essential to ensure the best use of the drain and to allow for unavoidable features such as trees, walls, etc., and to ensure that the drainage runs to a convenient outfall at an acceptable gradient. When used to drain fields or other agricultural land,

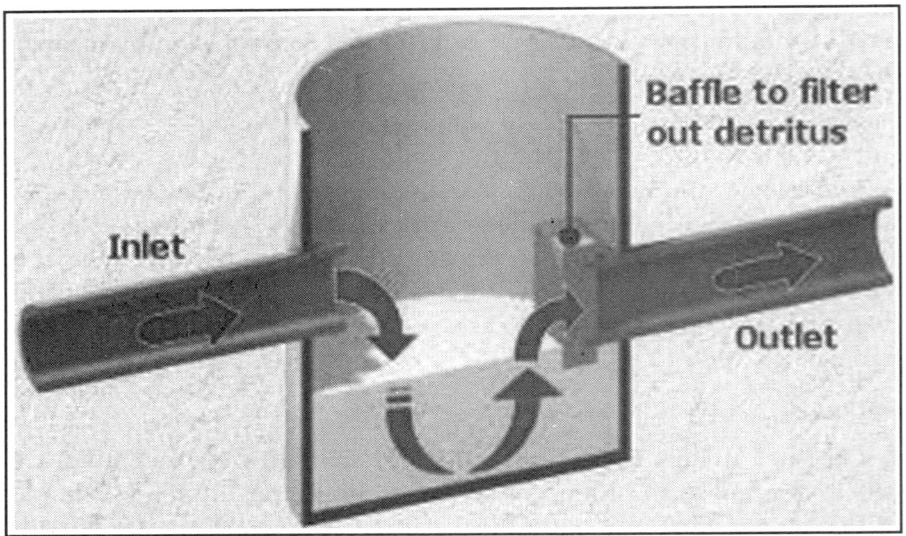

Fig. 3.6: Manufactured catchpit

the distance between individual drain runs can be 10 metres or more, depending on local conditions. Such systems are almost always installed by specialist contractors, often on behalf of the local water authority, and a full survey is usually undertaken before the ground is opened. Another use for land drainage in the garden is as a collector drain, installed as a single line, 300-450 mm from the edge of a pavement to carry away the surface run-off and prevent the garden from becoming water-logged. In this sort of scenario, a decorative gravel can be used to dress the surface of the drain, making it a feature of the hard landscaping.

Leach Fields

Dispersal systems, as used with septic tanks, normally discharge into a "Leach Field" (aka an 'absorption field'), a special area downstream of a septic tank where the treated effluent is allowed to soak into the ground whereupon the treatment process is continued by soil-borne bacteria and organisms. The size/area of the leach field is determined by the percolation rate of the ground and the number of persons served by the septic tank. Unlike collector drains, dispersal drains tend to be installed as 'closed' systems, ie, there are no 'dead end' lengths of pipe

Types of Pipes

Most land drainage systems consists of lengths of perforated or slotted plastic or clayware pipe laid in a trench with a porous surround. There is a wide range of sizes, from 80 mm flexible plastic, up to 1000 mm or more for large agricultural or commercial schemes, and they come in a wide variety of materials, including uPVC, clayware, fibre-cement, concrete and ductile iron.

Eighty mm diameter perforated flexible/corrugated plastic pipe (Fig. 3.7) is ideal for garden drainage. Larger diameters are also available and they are typically used on larger schemes, such as carriageway edge interceptor drains. The smaller flexible plastic type is readily available in 25m coils from your local builders' merchant at around £1-2 per metre. It is very simple to install, well within the capabilities of a DIY enthusiast. This type of land drain has holes or perforations around the entire circumference, so there is no 'top' or 'bottom'.

Fig. 3.7: Perforated Plastic

Rigid land drain pipes may be fabricated from clayware, plastic or other some other solid material. Some types will be perforated or slotted around the entire circumference while others will be 'half-perforated', ie, have holes on only one face of the pipe. As with their non-perforated cousins, rigid land drain pipes are normally joined together by means of a coupling, although some systems use 'sockets and spigots'.

There are a variety of different types of land drain available. Clayware and rigid plastic perforated pipes are generally more expensive than the flexible type and they should always be used where a land-drain passes beneath a trafficked area, such as a driveway, or where the depth of the drainage is such that the weight of the backfill material would cause a flexible plastic pipe to collapse. As a general rule of thumb, we do not use flexible plastic pipe at depths greater than 1.2 m.

Theoretically, a rigid perforated clayware land drain could be used at depths up to 6m, but this would require machine excavation and shoring, and is best left to professionals.

Land drainage systems rely on a combination of gravity and hydrostatic pressure to create a flow within the pipes. Systems are typically installed with a gentle slope in the region of 1:100-1:200 towards the outfall or disposal point. For this reason, it is best to lay land drainage 'uphill' i.e. start at the outfall, which should be the lowest point on the land drainage system.

The trench width is usually calculated as external pipe diameter (abbreviated to OD, as in Outside Diameter) plus 150 mm sidefill to each side, so, for a pipe with an OD of 115 mm, the trench width would need to be

$115 + (2 \times 150) = 415$ mm

The trench should be excavated in advance and lined with the geo-textile if one is to be used. The bedding material is placed in the base of the trench, then the pipe itself laid and checked for alignment and gradient before the sidefill is added and finally the backfill.

Ensure a clean gravel is used for the surrounding material, and do not use limestone chippings unless nothing else is available—Limestone can precipitate calcium carbonate in wet conditions, depositing minerals that can clog up the drain. Make sure there is at least 75 mm of gravel around and above the perforated pipe.

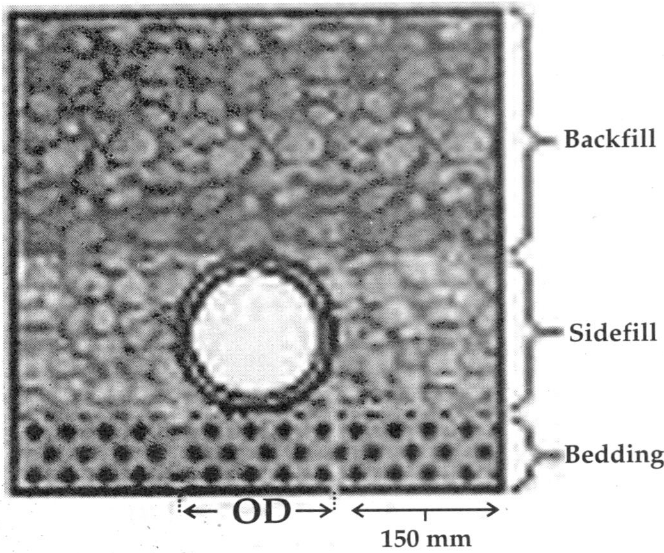

Fig. 3.8: FTrench sizing

The geo-textile filter is not essential, but will prolong the life of the drain by filtering out smaller clay and soil particles, and deter thirsty roots from seeking refreshment in the land drain. Small rootlets in a land drain can quickly expanded to a pipe-blocking mass!

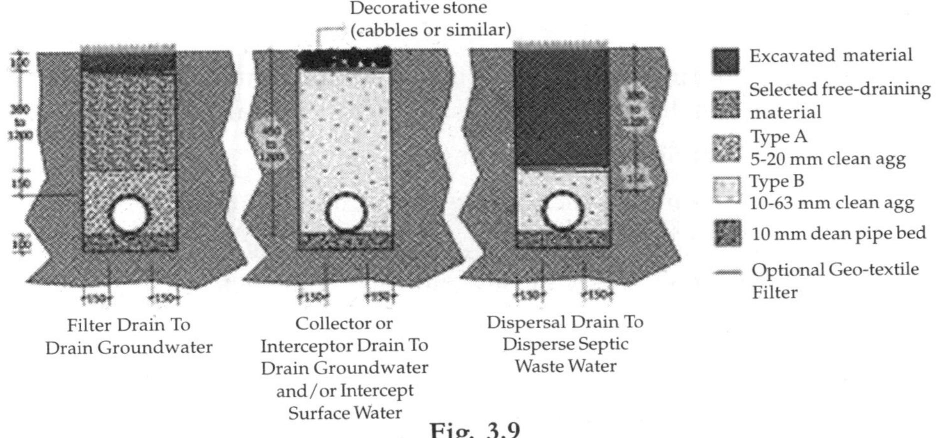

Fig. 3.9

Popularity of Drainage Trencher

The drainage trencher is probably the most popular machine for installing drainage pipes in all kinds of areas and climates. The principle allows accurate installation of the pipe and if required backfill material can easily be put over the drainage pipe. Apart from variations in size, there are two distinct types of drainage trenchers. Nowadays, the machine with a steep digging chain design is the most popular around the world but in certain areas the machine with a flat digging chain design has some major advantages in terms of accuracy and productivity.

Use of Drainage Plow

The drainage plow has become the most used machine for installing lateral drainage pipe. The most important reason for this is that it is cheaper than using trenching machines.Production is relatively high but machine running costs are low. This is an important reason and the fact the single blade is the least sensitive for underground obstacles has lead the plow to be the most popular machine for installing lateral drains.

V-plow Vs Single-blade Plow

The V-plow has some very distinct advantages over a single-blade plow and is therefore in some areas the only recognised machine for the trenchless installation of drainage pipe.

In the Netherlands, for example, 95 per cent of all plows are V-plows and the majority of farmers will not accept a single-blade plow in their fields. Other areas that have benefited positively from the use of V-plows include: parts of England, Belgium, some regions of the United States, Mexico, Egypt and India.

Advantages of the V-plow:

- Less deformation or compaction of the soil near the drain, especially when installation is carried out under the so-called "critical depth".
- Less smearing of the trench side.
- Better fissuring which aids water running to the pipe.
- High installation speeds at average depths of less that 5 feet. This advantage increases in clay and clay loam soils.
- Less damage to crops and soil surface.
- Less risk of piping in wet conditions.
- Minimal disruption to the surface so that levelling is not required after installation.
- As a result, use of the V-plow is cheaper than any other installation method.

Collector Drainage Pipe Installation

Collector drainage pipe installation can in principle be done by means of any of the above mentioned machines.

However for larger scale projects normally a large trencher with a steep digging chain design is used with an incorporated cross conveyor. These machines are normally better balanced to compensate for the large trench required and installation process. Mastenbroek has designed machines for some of the largest drainage projects in the world, including specific collector drainage machines for installing corrugated plastic pipes and for installation of concrete pipes by means of the Synchro Trench System.

4 Levelling and Topography

Levelling is a branch of surveying, the object of which is to find the elevation of a given point with respect to the given or assumed data. Secondly, it is to establish a point at a given elevation with respect to the given or assumed data.

Levelling is the measurement of geodetic height using an optical levelling instrument and a level staff or rod having a numbered scale. Common levelling instruments include the spirit level, the dumpy level, the digital level, and the laser level.

Spirit levelling employs a spirit level, an instrument consisting of a telescope and a tube level like that used by carpenters, rigidly connected. When the bubble in the tube level is in the middle, the telescope's optical axis (collimation axis) will point exactly in the direction of the local horizontal.

The spirit level is placed on a tripod in the middle between the two points whose height difference is to be determined; the points are marked by markers or benchmarks in the rock or soil. A levelling staff or rod is placed on each point, with measured graduations, usually in centimetres and fractions thereof, or tenths and hundredths of a foot. The observer focuses in turn on each rod and reads the value from it. Subtracting the "back" and "forward" value provides the height difference.

LEVELLING PROCEDURE AND INSTRUMENTS

A typical procedure is to set up the instrument within 100 metres (100 yards) of a known or assumed reference elevation point. A rod or staff is held on the point and the instrument is used either manually or automatically to read the rod scale as a backsight. This determines the height of the instrument above the point and allows the height of the instrument (H.I.) above the datum to be computed.

The rod is then held on an unknown point and a foresight reading is taken in the same manner, allowing the elevation of the new point to be computed. The procedure is repeated until the destination point is reached. It is usual practice to perform either a complete loop back to the starting point or else close the traverse on a second point whose elevation is already known. The closure check guards against blunders in the operation, and allows residual error to be distributed in the most likely manner among the stations.

Some instruments provide three crosshairs which allow stadia measurement of the foresight and backsight distances. These also allow use of the average of the three readings (3-wire levelling) as a check against blunders and for averaging out the error of interpolation between marks on the rod scale.

In double-levelling, a surveyor takes two foresights and two backsights and makes sure the difference between the foresights and the difference between the backsights are equal, thereby reducing the amount of error. Double-levelling costs twice as much as single-levelling.

Dumpy Level

The dumpy level is an older style of optical instrument. It is commonly believed that dumpy levelling is less accurate than other types of levelling, but such is not the case. Dumpy levelling requires shorter and therefore more numerous sights, but this fault is compensated by the practice of making foresights and backsights equal.

The Wye level is another older style of instrument, whose operation is similar to that of the dumpy level. Precise Level designs were often used for large leveling projects where utmost accuracy was required. They differ from other levels in having a very precise spirit level tube and a micrometer adjustment to raise or lower the line of sight so that the crosshair can be made to coincide with a line on the rod scale and no interpolation is required.

Automatic Level

Automatic levels make use of a compensator, which ensures that the line of sight is always horizontal regardless of whether or not the housing of the telescope is. This makes it easier and quicker to set-up than a tilting or dumpy level. It also reduces the effect of minor settling of the tripod to the actual amount of motion instead of leveraging the tilt over the sight distance. These instruments became standard in the later part of the twentieth century where three level screws are given to adjust the instrument level.

Digital Level

Digital levels electronically read a bar-coded scale on the staff. These instruments usually include data recording capability. The automation removes the requirement for the operator to read a scale and and write down the value, and so reduces blunders. It may also compute and apply refraction and curvature corrections.

Laser Level

Laser levels project a beam which is visible and/or detectable by a sensor on the leveling rod. This style is widely used in construction work but not for more precise control work. An advantage is that one person can perform the levelling independently, whereas other types require one person at the instrument and one holding the rod.

The sensor can be mounted on earth-moving machinery to allow automated grading.

Topography is the study of Earth's surface shape and features or those of planets, moons, and asteroids. It is also the description of such surface shapes and features (especially their depiction in maps). The topography of an area can also mean the surface shape and features themselves. In a broader sense, topography is concerned with local detail in general, including not only relief but also vegetative and human-made features, and even local history and culture. This meaning is less common in America, where topographic maps with elevation contours have made "topography" synonymous with relief. The older sense of topography as the study of place still has currency in Europe.

Topography specifically involves the recording of relief or terrain, the three-dimensional quality of the surface, and the identification of specific landforms. This is also known as geomorpho-metry. In modern usage, this involves generation of elevation data in electronic form. It is often considered to include the graphic representation of the landform on a map by a variety of techniques, including contour lines, Hypsometric tints, and relief shading.

An objective of topography is to determine the position of any feature or more generally any point in terms of both a horizontal coordinate system such as latitude, longitude, and altitude. Identifying (naming) features and recognizing typical landform patterns are also part of the field.

A topographic study may be made for a variety of reasons: military planning and geological exploration have been primary motivators to start survey programmes, but detailed information about terrain and surface features is essential for the planning and construction of any major civil engineering, public works, or reclamation projects.

The term 'topography' originated in ancient Greece and continued in ancient Rome, as the detailed description of a place. The word comes from the Greek words ('topos', place) and ('graphia', writing). In classical literature, this refers to writing about a place or places, what is now largely called 'local history'. In Britain and in Europe in general, the word topography is still sometimes used in its original sense.

Detailed military surveys in Britain (beginning in the late eighteenth century) were called Ordnance Surveys, and this term was used into the 20th century as generic for topographic surveys and maps.The earliest scientific surveys in France were called the Cassini maps after the family who produced them over four generations.

The term "topographic surveys" appears to be American in origin. The earliest detailed surveys in the United States were made by the "Topographical Bureau of the Army," formed during the War of 1812. After the work of national mapping was assumed by the U.S. Geological Survey in 1878, the term topographical remained as a general term for detailed surveys and mapping programmes, and has been adopted by most other nations as standard.

In the 20th century, the term topography started to be used to describe surface description in other fields where mapping in a broader sense is used, particularly in medical fields such as neurology.

TECHNIQUES OF TOPOGRAPHY

There are a variety of approaches to studying topography. Which method(s) to use depend on the scale and size of the area under study, its accessibility, and the quality of existing surveys.

Fig. 4.1: A surveying point in Germany

Direct Survey

Surveying helps determine accurately the terrestrial or three-dimensional space position of points and the distances and angles between them using levelling instruments such as theodolites, dumpy levels and clinometers.

Even though remote sensing has greatly sped up the process of gathering information, and has allowed greater accuracy control over long distances, the direct survey still provides the basic control points and framework for all topographic work, whether manual or GIS-based.

In areas where there has been an extensive direct survey and mapping programme (most of Europe and the Continental US, for example), the compiled data forms the basis of basic digital elevation datasets such as USGS DEM data. This data must often be "cleaned" to eliminate discrepancies between surveys, but it still forms a valuable set of information for large-scale analysis.

The original American topographic surveys (or the British "Ordnance" surveys) involved not only recording of relief, but identification of landmark features and vegetative land cover.

Remote sensing is the acquisition of information about an object or phenomenon, without making physical contact with the object. In modern usage, the term generally refers to the use of aerial sensor technologies to detect and classify objects on Earth (both on the surface, and in the atmosphere and oceans) by means of propagated signals.

AERIAL PHOTOGRAPHY

Aerial photography is the taking of photographs of the ground from an elevated position. The term usually refers to images in which the camera is not supported by a ground-based structure. Cameras may be hand held or mounted, and photographs may be taken by a photo-grapher, triggered remotely or triggered automatically. Platforms for aerial photography include fixed-wing aircraft, helicopters, balloons, blimps and dirigibles, rockets, kites, poles, parachutes, vehicle mounted poles . Aerial photography should not be confused with Air-to-Air Photography, when aircraft serve both as a photo platform and subject.

Uses of Imagery

Aerial photography is used in cartography (particularly inphotogrammetric surveys, which are often the basis fortopographic maps), land-use planning, archaeology, movie production, environmental studies, surveillance, commercial advertising, conveyancing and artistic projects.

Radio-controlled Aircraft

Advances in radio controlled models have made it possible for model aircraft to conduct low-altitude aerial photography. This has benefited real-estate advertising, where commercial and residential properties are the photographic subject. Full-size, manned aircraft are prohibited from low flights above populated locations.

Small scale model aircraft offer increased photographic access to these previously restricted areas. Miniature vehicles do not replace full size aircraft, as full size aircraft are capable of longer flight times, higher altitudes, and greater equipment payloads. They are, however, useful in any situation in which a full-scale aircraft would be dangerous to operate. Examples would include the inspection of transformers atop power transmission lines and slow, low-level flight over agricultural fields, both of which can be accomplished by a large-scale radio controlled helicopter. Professional-grade, gyroscopically stabilized camera platforms are available for use under such a model; a large model helicopter with a 26cc gasoline engine can hoist a payload of approximately seven kilograms (15 lbs).

The FAA regulations grounding all commercial RC model flights have been upgraded to require formal FAA certification before permission to fly at any altitude in USA.

Because anything capable of being viewed from a public space is considered outside the realm of privacy in the United States, aerial photography may legally document features and occurrences on private property.

Types of Aerial Photographs

Oblique Photographs

Photographs taken at an angle are called oblique photographs. If they are taken from a low angle earth surface–aircraft, they are called low oblique and photo-graphs taken from a high angle are called high or steep oblique.

Vertical Photographs

Vertical photographs are taken straight down. They are mainly used in photogrammetry and image interpretation. Pictures that will be used in photogrammetry are traditionally taken with special large format cameras with calibrated and documented geometric properties.

Combinations

Aerial photographs are often combined. Depending on their purpose it can be done in several ways, of which a few are listed below:

- Panoramas can be made by stitching several photographs taken with one hand held camera.
- In pictometry five rigidly mounted cameras provide one vertical and four low oblique pictures that can be used together.
- In some digital cameras for aerial photogrammetry images from several imaging elements, sometimes with separate lenses, are geometrically corrected and combined to one image in the camera.

Fig. 4.2: Pteryx UAV, a civilian UAV for aerial photography and photomapping with roll-stabilised camera head

Orthophotos

Vertical photographs are often used to create orthophotos, photographs which have been geometrically "corrected" so as to be usable as a map. In other words, an orthophoto is a simulation of a photograph taken from an infinite distance, looking straight down from nadir. Perspective must obviously be removed, but variations in terrain should also be corrected for. Multiple geometric transformations are applied to the image, depending on the perspective and terrain corrections required on a particular part of the image.

Orthophotos are commonly used in geographic information systems, such as are used by mapping agencies to create maps. Once the images have been aligned, or 'registered', with known real-world coordinates, they can be widely deployed.

Large sets of orthophotos, typically derived from multiple sources and divided into "tiles" (each typically 256 × 256 pictures in size), are widely used in online map systems such as Google Maps. OpenStreetMap offers the use of similar orthophotos for deriving new map data. Google Earthoverlays orthophotos or satellite imagery onto a digital elevation model to simulate 3D landscapes.

Satellite imagery consists of photographs of Earth or other planets made by means of artificial satellites.

The first images from space were taken on sub-orbital flights. The U.S-launched V-2 flight on October 24, 1946 took one image every 1.5 seconds. With an apogee of 65 miles (105 km), these photos were from five times higher than the previous record, the 13.7 miles (22 km) by the Explorer II balloon mission in 1935.

The first satellite (orbital) photographs of Earth were made on August 14, 1959 by the U.S. Explorer 6. The first satellite photographs of the Moon might have been made on October 6, 1959 by the Soviet satellite Luna 3, on a mission to photograph the far side of the Moon. The Blue Marble photograph was taken from space in 1972, and has become very popular in the media and among the public. Also in 1972 the United States started the Landsat programme, the largest programme for acquisition of imagery of Earth from space. Landsat 7, the most recent Landsat satellite, was launched in 1999. In 1977, the first real time satellite imagery was acquired by the USA's KH-11 satellite system.

All satellite images produced by NASA are published by Earth Observatory and are freely available to the public. Several other countries have satellite imaging programmes, and a collaborative European effort launched the ERS and Envisat satellites carrying various sensors. There are also private companies that provide commercial satellite imagery. In the early 21st century satellite imagery became widely available when affordable, easy to use software with access to satellite imagery databases became offered by several companies and organizations.

Fig. 4.3: Satellite photography can be used to produce composite images of an entire hemisphere

Uses

Satellite images have many applications in meteorology, agriculture, geology, forestry, biodiversity conservation, regional planning, education, intelligence and warfare. Images can be in visible colours and in other spectra. There are also elevation maps, usually made by radar imaging. Interpretation and analysis of satellite imagery is conducted using software packages like ERDAS Imagine or ENVI.

Some of the first image enhancement of satellite photos was conducted by the U.S. Government and its contractors. For example ESL Incorporateddeveloped some of the earliest two dimensionalFourier transforms applied to digital image processing to address NASA photos as well asnational security applications. Satellite imagery is also used in seismology and oceanography in deducing changes to land formation, water depth and sea bed, by colour caused by earthquakes,volcanoes, and tsunamis.

Resolution and Data

There are four types of resolution when discussing satellite imagery in remote sensing: spatial, spectral, temporal, and radiometric. Researcher defines these as follows:

- Spatial resolution is defined as the pixel size of an image representing the size of the surface area being measured on the ground, determined by the sensors' instantaneous field of view (IFOV);
- Spectral resolution is defined by the wavelength interval size (discreet segment of the Electromagnetic Spectrum) and number intervals that the sensor is measuring; temporal resolution is defined by the amount of time (i.e. days) that passes between imagery collection periods; and radiometric resolution is defined as the ability of an imaging system to record many levels of brightness (contrast for example);
- Radiometric resolution refers to the effective bit-depth of the sensor (number of greyscale levels) and is typically expressed as 8-bit (0-255), 11-bit (0-2047), 12-bit (0-4095) or 16-bit (0-65,535);
- Geometric resolution refers to the satellite sensor's ability to effectively image a portion of the Earth's surface in a single pixel and is typically expressed in terms of Ground Sample Distance, or GSD. GSD is a term containing the overall optical and systemic noise sources and is useful for comparing how well one sensor can "see" an object on the ground within a single pixel. For example, the GSD of Landsat is nearly 30m, which means the smallest unit

that maps to a single pixel within an image is ~30m × 30m. The latest commercial satellite (GeoEye 1) has a GSD of 0.41 m (effectively 0.5 m due to US Government restrictions on civilian imaging).

The resolution of satellite images varies depending on the instrument used and the altitude of the satellite's orbit. For example, the Landsat archive offers repeated imagery at 30 metre resolution for the planet, but most of it has not been processed from the raw data. Landsat 7 has an average return period of 16 days. For many smaller areas, images with resolution as high as 41 cm can be available.

Satellite imagery is sometimes supplemented with aerial photography, which has higher resolution, but is more expensive per square meter. Satellite imagery can be combined with vector or raster data in a GIS provided that the imagery has been spatially rectified so that it will properly align with other data sets.

Disadvantages

Because the total area of the land on Earth is so large and because resolution is relatively high, satellite databases are huge and image processing (creating useful images from the raw data) is time-consuming. Depending on the sensor used, weather conditions can affect image quality: for example, it is difficult to obtain images for areas of frequent cloud cover such as mountain-tops.

Commercial satellite companies do not place their imagery into the public domain and do not sell their imagery; instead, one must be licensed to use their imagery. Thus, the ability to legally make derivative products from commercial satellite imagery is minimized.

Privacy concerns have been brought up by some who wish not to have their property shown from above. Google Maps responds to such concerns in their FAQ with the following statement: "We understand your privacy concerns. The images that Google Maps displays are no different from what can be seen by anyone who flies over or drives by a specific geographic location."

Photogrammetry

Photogrammetry is a measurement technique for which the co-ordinates of the points in 3D of an object are determined by the measurements made in two photo-graphic images (or more) taken starting from different positions, usually from different passes of an aerial photography flight. In this technique, the common points are identified on each image. A line of sight (or ray) can be built from the camera location to the point on the object.

It is the intersection of its rays (triangulation) which determines the relative three-dimensional position of the point. Known control points can be used to give these relative positions absolute values. More sophisticated algorithms can exploit other information on the scene known a priori (for example, symmetries in certain cases allowing the rebuilding of three-dimensional co-ordinates starting from one only position of the camera).

Radar and Sonar

Satellite radar mapping is one of the major techniques of generating Digital Elevation Models. Similar techniques are applied in bathymetric surveys using sonar to determine the terrain of the ocean floor. In recent years, LIDAR (Light Detection and Ranging), a remote sensing technique using a laser instead of radio waves, has increasingly been employed for complex mapping needs such as charting canopies and monitoring glaciers.

Forms of Topographic Data

Terrain is commonly modelled either using vector (triangulated irregular network or TIN) or gridded (Raster image) mathematical models. In the most applications in environmental sciences, land surface is represented and modelled using gridded models. In civil engineering and entertainment businesses, the most representations of land surface employ some variant of TIN models. In geostatistics, land surface is commonly modelled as a combination of the two signals—the smooth (spatially correlated) and the rough (noise) signal.

In practice, surveyors first sample heights in an area, then use these to produce a Digital Land Surface Model (DLSM) (also known as a digital elevation model). The DLSM can then be used to visualize terrain, drape remote sensing images, quantify ecological properties of a surface or extract land surface objects. Note that the contour data or any other sampled elevation datasets are not a DLSM.

A DLSM implies that elevation is available continuously at each location in the study area, i.e. that the map represents a complete surface. Digital Land Surface Models should not be confused with Digital Surface Models, which can be surfaces of the canopy, buildings and similar objects.

For example, in the case of surface models produces using the LIDAR technology, one can have several surfaces—starting from the top of the canopy to the actual solid earth. The difference between the two surface models can then be used to derive volumetric measures (height of trees etc.).

Raw Survey Data

Topographic survey information is historically based upon the notes of surveyors. They may derive naming and cultural information from other local sources (for example, boundary delineation may be derived from local cadastral mapping. While of historical interest, these field notes inherently include errors and contradictions that later stages in map production resolve.

Remote Sensing Data

As with field notes, remote sensing data as aerial and satellite photography, is raw and uninterpreted. It may contain holes (due to cloud cover for example or inconsis-tencies (due to the timing of specific image captures). Most modern topographic mapping includes a large component of remotely sensed data in its compilation process.

Fig. 4.4: A map of Europe usingelevation modeling

Topographic Mapping

In its contemporary definition, topographic mapping shows relief. In the United States, USGS topographic maps show relief using contour lines. The USGS calls maps based on topographic surveys, but without contours, "planimetric maps."

These maps show not only the contours, but also any significant streams or other bodies of water, forest cover, built-up areas or individual buildings (depending on scale), and other features and points of interest.

While not officially "topographic" maps, the national surveys of other nations share many of the same features, and so they are often generally called "topographic maps".

Existing topographic survey maps, because of their comprehensive and encyclopedic coverage, form the basis for much derived topographic work. Digital Elevation Models, for example, have often been created not from new remote sensing data but from existing paper topographic maps. Many government and private publishers use the artwork especially the contour lines from existing topographic map sheets as the basis for their own specialized or updated topographic maps·

Topographic mapping should not be confused with Geologic mapping. The latter is concerned with underlying structures and processes to the surface, rather than with identifiable surface features.

5 Laying Out Drains in the Field

The soil around the drain is the driest point in winter and wettest point in summer—hence the dark green colour in the turf.

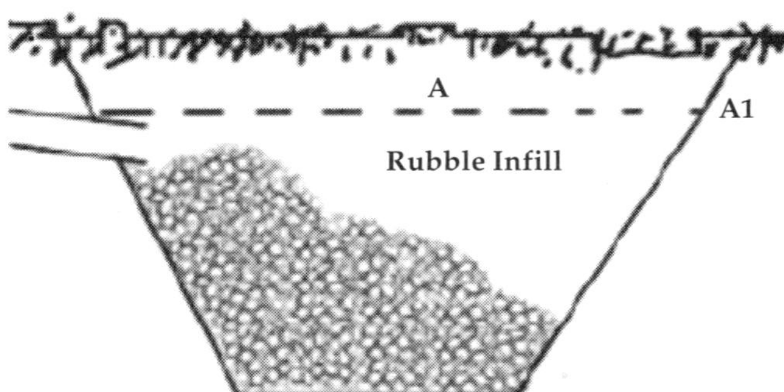

Fig. 5.1: Sloping sided for safegy

LAYING LAND DRAINS

Laying a land drain, or French drain is the easiest method of dealing with surplus water in your garden. Perforated plastic drainage pipe (80mm) can now be bought from many garden centres and all builders merchants in 25 rolls. This type of pipe is easily laid in small trenches and surrounded by shingle (small stones) to allow water through but filter out silt. The pipe can be joined using a waterproof repair tape also available from builder's merchants.

Land Drain Pipe can also be bought in clay sections but the introduction of plastic has made their use, for the domestic application, virtually obsolete. Pipe can also be bought which only has holes half way round. This, for drainage purposes, is laid with the holes uppermost to allow water in from the surface and then to allow it to get carried away completely. We do not advocate the use of this in an English Garden as a fully perforated pipe will allow a more even distribution of the water from wetter, to drier parts, on its journey to the outlet.

With the introduction of what is commonly called Weed Fabric into the market place, it is now possible to wrap the pipe in weed fabric which should stop any silt getting into the pipe. Many builders, ourselves included, actually line the trench with Weed Fabric or Geo Textile Fabric to give it its proper name, to stop any silt getting into the trench. This gives the land drain a much longer life as silt can build up in a matter of weeks and clog all of the voids which are vital to proper drainage.

The Geo Textile Fabric will also stop, or at least dissuade, any local roots seeking out a greater water source. A root system can clog or even break a land drain system quite easily. Geo Textile fabric is a polypropylene mat used to suppress weeds and control soil erosion while allowing the controlled passage of water and air.

Land Drains and French drains can also be used to direct water to a part of your garden which needs more water than others. This is particularly useful for gardeners. A French Drain is simply a land drain but without the pipe although this terminology is getting somewhat mixed these days with many people referring to Land Drains as French Drains.

Land drains in gardens are usually drained to a central point and this is usually a soakaway. A soakaway is simply a hole in the ground filled with rubble and coarse stone with a drainage pipe laid to it removing surface (rain) water from other areas. The soil in which the soakaway is placed must be granular with good drainage properties. It is pointless sinking a soakaway in clay unless there is a more porous layer underneath. The diagram below is not to scale.

A soakaway must be at least five metres from any habitable building, by local authority regulations. The pipe flowing to them should be of at least 75 mm diameter which is the minimum pipe size for any surface water drainage. 80 mm is the recommended size.

This pipe should be laid to a fall of 1 in 100 which means for every one m of pipe length the slope should be about 10 mm or one cm. However gradual the slope, water will find its way down it.

The size of the soakaway should be a minimum of 1m × 1m square × 1m deep below the bottom of the incoming pipe. The stone infill should surround the pipe and finish approximately 100 smm above it. An impervious layer should then be placed on the stone such as thick polythene, tarpaulin, or even a bed of concrete. Topsoil can then be placed on top of this layer to restore the garden level (A). If you can afford it we also suggest lining the soakaway with weed fabric. As the soakaway needs to be 1m deep below the bottom of the incoming land drain it makes sense to measure the distance of the land drain you intend to lay and work out, using the fall of 1:100, how deep the bottom of the pipe will be when it gets to the soakaway.

For example, if your soakaway is to be placed at the bottom of the garden and your garden is 30m long, the pipe will be 300 mm deeper when it gets to the soakaway. If the pipe starts in a trench 300mm deep the bottom of the pipe will be 600mm below the ground when it gets to the soakaway. This means, in total, your soakaway is 1600mm or 1.6m deep.

Care should be taken when digging a hole this deep and we suggest digging the sides back at a fairly shallow angle to avoid any of the sides caving in. Wet soil weighs over 1 tonne per cubic meter and it is extremely dangerous to carry out any excavation over 600mm deep without either shoring up the sides of the trench or raking (digging at an angle) them back. There are no rules to say that a soakaway has to be a perfect cube and your safety is more important than the few extra barrow loads of rubble required to fill a bigger hole.

For turf used in sports, the aim is not merely to remove surplus water, but to remove it quickly enough to allow play as soon as possible. This involves:

- The provision of a drainage system.
- Ensuring the water gets through the soil to the drainage system.

The Benefits of Good Drainage

- Removal of excess water and lowering the water table.
- Improves the quality, firmness and durability of the turf, especially for winter games.
- Quick drying of the soil extending possible playing time.
- Prevention of erosion.
- Prevention of heaving.
- Improved air movement in soils.
- Increased root development.

- Increased capillary moisture in dry weather.
- Improved drought resistance.
- Better soil structure.
- Higher soil temperature and longer growing season.
- Improved bacterial action.

Kinds of Drainage Systems

(a) Open drains or ditches.

(b) Pipe drains.

(c) Mole drains.

(d) French drains.

Water on Surface

The cause of the cancelled match or the playing of a match in bad ground conditions is usually because of the water on the surface or in the surface layer of top soil. It takes time for water to penetrate the soil surface and enter drains that are several feet down, so at this point sports field drainage requirements differ from that of the farmer and agriculture, although the basic points are still applicable, such as the laying of pipes, junctions, falls etc.

Types of Drain for Sportsfields

Mole Plough Draining: effective but limited life and the mole cuts must be lined to either a ditch or a drain of some sort - pull mole uphill - clay type soil required: winch pulled mole and/or mole plough fitted direct to tractor on three point linkage. Plough follows ground levels - time of year to carry out work and when not to!

Drains-Clay, Porous Concrete, Perforated Plastic: I prefer to use clay - up to now I have not been impressed with the results of plastic pipes that I have seen laid.

Clay Tiles: For normal work: 3″ dia. 4″ dia. 6″ dia. Plus necessary junction: always use a salt-glazed pipe or similar 3′ long at outlet into water course or if connected to storm water system. You have no right of discharge into a surface water sewer. If you get permission to do this you will have to fit a silt trap prior to entry into the sewer, also concrete the face of your outlet into a water course to prevent water undermining it.

Porous Concrete : These drainage pipes can be used except in sulphate-bearing clays such as Gault and London clay. Both contain sulphate and the use of porous concrete drains in these areas is not recommended.

Perforated Plastic: These are now the most widely used pipes for land drainage work. They come in a wide range of sizes - 1½" to 4" - and in lengths of 12 to 20 feet or in large coils. The lengths have a male and female end so that they are easily fitted together. The coils have a sleeve fitting for linking sections together. Because they conduct water more 'smoothly' than clay pipes, a smaller diameter pipe - i.e. 1½" dia. can carry as much drainage water as a 3' clay pipe set at the small rate of fall. This also means that drainage trenches can be narrow, resulting in the removal of backfilling material. They are also lighter to handle and transport than clay and concrete tiles.

NATURAL DRAINAGE

Some soils are well-drained, others easily waterlogged. As rain falls on the turf some evaporates, some may run off and the rest passes into the ground to become soil water. Some of this is absorbed by the plants' roots and is passed back into the atmosphere by transpiration. The rest passes on down until it reaches the level of the water table or an impermeable layer of soil or rock strata. It then commences to form a water table. Water table rises during the winter and falls during the summer. Sandstone is porous and these types or soil are naturally well-drained. Clay-type soils when dry can absorb up to 50% of their bulk in water (like blotting paper), but once this water has been absorbed the clay becomes impermeable and water cannot pass through it.

Excess Water

This means inadequate aeration, lower soil temperature—as much as 12°F degrees between drained and undrained soils. A high water table limits the range of roots. Insufficient air and low temperature slows down the decomposition of organic matter in the soil; and to the groundsman cancelled matches or the destruction of the soil structure if play is allowed to take place, this in turn means difficulty in renovating and establishing new turf during the close season.

The reduction of the height of the water table if closer than two feet to the soil surface will enable grass roots to reach their maximum depth. In turn, this improves aeration and mechanical equipment can be used to assist this. Also raises the soil temperature.

The ground and turf are less likely to suffer drought conditions in the summer for it is a fact that in wet weather the driest soil is to be found around the drain, yet in dry weather the soil around the drain has the greatest moisture content.

Drainage Systems

Natural

Where drains follow natural contours, not usually of use in large sports ground work, possibly of use in light soils or on small areas.

Herringbone

Gives short lengths to the lateral drains. More complicated for machine working and the many junctions increase the danger of silting.

Grid System

Easy for machine working. Long laterals. Size of clay drain up to half to half an acre at a fall of 1-300-3″. If fall increased the larger areas can be dealt with. After this 4″ pipes then use 6″ mains unless rate of fall of the main is increased. In laying out a system the aim should be to set the laterals at an angle to the slope so acting as interceptors to the flow of water. Also cut off interceptor drains at banks etc.

Depth of Drains

The outfall - this is usually the governing factor. It should be as deep as possible subject to reason. It should be above the normal level of a watercourse, so as to give unimpeded flow, but deep enough to allow for drains to reach the farthest part of the system at a depth of at least 12″ (preferably 18″). In allowing for this, also allow for a fall from lateral drains into main drains. Also, it is generally accepted that the main should fall quicker than the lateral drains to prevent silting and this is also necessary if the same size dia. pipes are used. However, if it is difficult to get sufficient fall then the mains should be of larger size and silt traps built. These can be cleaned out when necessary. There is a rough rule of thumb that for every 1" of depth, the drain will pull for 1 foot on each side: more in light soil, less in heavy. This gives a rough guide to the distance apart of the laterals.

The Fall

This can be as steep as 1-50 if necessary. However, 1-75 is normally regarded as ideal although it can be 1-300, or if dealing with very large areas then 1-600. The important points to bear in mind are that the drain runs are straight and constant in their fall.

The Trench

Nothing is gained in taking out a trench wider than is necessary, i.e. a 4″ trench for a 3″ pipe. It is a fallacy that more water will enter the pipe by having a trench wider than is necessary to get the pipe into it. The base of the trench should be 'boned' to ensure that there is a constant even fall.

Laying the Pipes

There are two schools of thought:

- Lay the pipes with a slight gap between each pipe not more than 1/8″.
- Lay the pipes as close together as possible, i.e. butt the ends tightly to each other.

Back Filling

It should be not more than 1½″ and smaller if possible. Backfilling should go to within 3-4″ of the surface and a binding of fine ash or pea shingle over the top. Then fill with good top soil and either turf or sand.

New Idea

Above the pipe put a 2-3″ layer of 3/8″ shingle, fill trench with dune sand to within a few inches of the surface, then use light top soil. The idea is that the shingle acts as a valve and once water falls on the surface, so that the dune sand is at field- capacity, then the excess immediately passes from the dune sand into the shingle and then to the drain. The idea is to provide instant drainage yet enable sufficient water to be held in the sand to provide against drought conditions in summer.

The soil around the drain is the driest point in winter and wettest point in summer - hence the dark green colour in the turf.

Laying the Land Drains

To ensure that all applicable parts of your garden are drained, the most effective method of laying land drainsis to lay them in a herring bone pattern. The pipes should be laid so that no point in the garden is any more than 2 m away from a pipe. The maximum distance between pipes is therefore, 4 m. The centre line, or spine, of the drain takes the water to the soakaway and all of the other lines, or ribs, feed into the spine. To set this formation out it is as well to buy a bag of sand and, after measuring the distances involved, sprinkle sand down each line of pipe you want to insert.

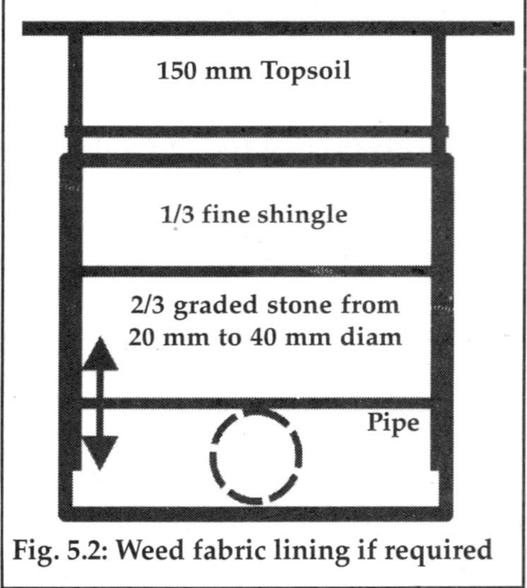

Fig. 5.2: Weed fabric lining if required

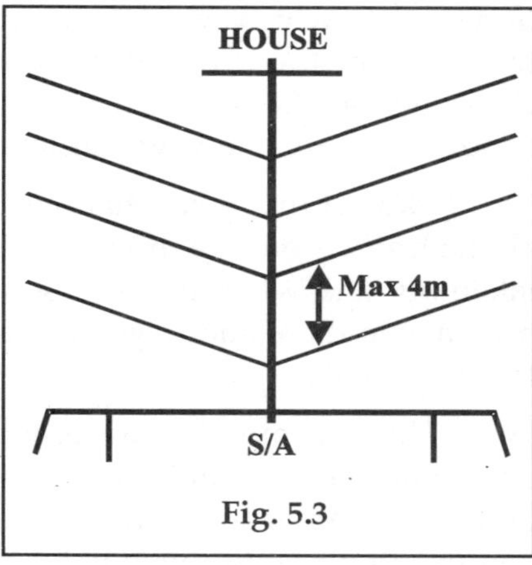

Fig. 5.3

Excavation of the trenches should ensure that any turf is cut carefully and stored to be re-laid later. Dig the trenches three times the width of the pipe to the required gentle fall to get the water to the soakaway or outlet.

After lining the trench with weed fabric, lay the pipe in the centre. Surround the pipe with small stone which is available from the builder's merchants and garden centres. Clean stone with an average diameter of 20 mm is fine.

When the pipe is surrounded by an equal thickness of stone, i.e. there should be a top covering of stone equal to, or greater than the side covering, the weed fabric should be folded over the top. At least 150 mm of topsoil is then replaced to lay your turf on. This area can then be rolled to assist with regrowth.

FRENCH DRAINS

A cheaper method of achieving land drainage which is, historically, used to remove surface water from the perimeter of a house or patio, is a French drain.

A French drain is a Land drain without the pipe. It is excavated in the same way, filled with stone in the same way and backfilled in the same way. The construction only differs in so much as it is much more important, with a French Drain, to excavate the bottom of the trench to the exact slope required all the way to the outlet. With a land drain there is a certain amount of flexibility in so much as the pipe level can be adjusted by some of the bedding. One further word of warning is required here.

The land drains or French Drains you have put in, are there to remove water from areas of your garden. When laid properly they will still be doing this in drier spells and can cause parts of the garden, especially in prolonged dry spells, to scorch. You may notice the lines of the land drains as staying greener and more lush much longer as this is where the water is! The drainage system was necessary to breathe new life into the property that had been dug up and later refilled.

A portion of the Olson Farm in Willmar, Minnesota about 100 miles west of Minneapolis was used to supply fill for a local highway project. A few years later, in late 2006, this soil was replaced by a half a million yards of black dirt from a business park. "The farm property had a lot of clay underneath, which was taken out to build the four-lane highway, lowering the grade of the property by three feet," explained Vreeman of Vreeman Construction, "so black dirt was brought back to rebuild the field. It took about a year for the new soil to settle."

It was at this point that he started on the drainage system. "Because of all the traffic from the dump trucks packing down the soil both when it was taken out and when the new soil was put in, it was important to get good drainage in there and to get air back into the soil to promote root growth on this property.

"The system will allow any excess water that comes through the soil to drain into the pipe and then off the farm. This keeps the soil moisture at an optimum." Water from the farm moves through the tiling system into a ditch and eventually into the Hawk Creek watershed.

"First, we put in a 12-inch smooth wall pipe in December 2007 that would act as the main," Vreeman explained. "Then, in the spring of 2008 after the soil was drier, we put in the corrugated high-density polyethylene pipe that most call 'seepage tile'. There were a lot of quarter-mile long runs so it went very quickly with the pipe coming directly off the coils that held more than a half-mile of pipe. We put in and connected these runs to the 12-inch main in one day. All 40 acres were planted with corn that same day. We actually started at six in the morning and the planter came in at four o'clock."

The drainage system is set on a grid pattern and consists of the 12-inch main outlet lines, and 24,000 feet of four-inch pipe to collect the seepage. Some eightand six-inch diameter corrugated pipe was also used. The pipe, connections and fittings were manufactured and supplied by Prinsco. The company's environmentally sustainable ECOFLO® corrugated HDPE pipe was used for the 12-inch mainline.

"What's unique about our ECOFLO pipe is that it is manufactured using a blend of material containing a minimum of 50 per cent recycled HDPE," explained Joe Larkins, director of quality for Prinsco. "There is a great deal of technology and scrutiny that goes into our polymer science and manufacturing operations to assure that our customers receive environmentally conscious products with unparalleled performance. Their product is manufactured with recycled materials targeting a 30-hour Notched Constant Ligament Stress (NCLS) value to ensure superior resistance to cracking and a long service life.

Prinsco's GOLDLINE® corrugated HDPE pipe provided the required perforation pattern for the subsurface drainage. The 4-inch diameter pipe was delivered to the farm in 3000 foot-long coils. Geotextile wrap was not required and installation was done with a self-contained plow, eliminating the need for a more expensive and time consuming cut and cover operation. The all important grid pattern for the drainage system was mapped-out by Bonnema Surveys. The most critical factor is a good outlet for the water. Every piece of land lies differently and we strive to lay out the pipe system in such a way that it maximizes the productivity and crop yield of the acreage.

That property was a little different than most because they covered about 80 per cent of the farm with the seepage system. This land has a few low spots where water will stand, but it's fairly flat. And that makes the layout all the more important. They designed the system to maximize the grade, which leads to a longlife, healthy drainage system. This gives the farmer higher yields, greater crop margins and increases the enjoyment of farming.

Proper soil drainage is one of the most important success factors for a farm from both an environmental and productivity level. It started out nearly 200 years ago with foot-long clay tiles laid by hand to manage the subsurface water. As technology evolved it quickly became apparent that flexible and durable pipe made from high-density polyethylene could be made in coils of several thousand feet. This would not only permit a system to have optimum water flow and maximize crop productivity, but would also be quick to install and last for a very long time.

HDPE pipe is also versatile enough to be manufactured with various perforation patterns. This enables water to drain from the soil no matter what the contour or condition of the field may be and without diminishing the performance or longevity of the pipe.

Surveyor and drainage layout expert Bonnema said "This was a typical project. We went in and took some preliminary elevations to see how to best utilize the natural grade of the farm land to insure a long-lasting functional layout of corrugated polyethylene pipe under the property. Basically, what we're doing is giving the farm land three feet of non-saturated and aerated soil so that the crops will be healthy and productive.

We've been laying out drainage tile systems for about 30 years. The biggest change is that when we started it was all foot-long concrete tiles laid end to end. Then the corrugated HDPE pipe came along and completely took over the market. It's just a wonderful product. You rarely have a washout.

This was a major problem for farmers, according to Bonnema, especially in Minnesota. "Washouts were a big maintenance headache in the old days. If the frost action or shifting soil caused damage to one of those foot-long concrete tiles, the storm runoff water would eventually dig out a sink hole and a couple of yards of top soil would end up flowing down into the tile system, clogging the tile. And that would have to be dug up and repaired.

You won't have that problem with HDPE pipe because it's a continuous pipe. Plus it's a much easier product to ship to the field and install. If it's installed properly it will last many, many years. Known for the coldest winters in the nation, the frostline is also a concern.

Prinsco has been producing drainage solutions for the agricultural, construction and landscaping industries since 1975. Based in Minnesota, it has facilities in the Midwest and the west coast. Prinsco is a PPI member company and part of the Institute's corrugated plastic pipe division.

6 Fixing the Grade of Drains

Every yard lies at a slight, or sharp, angle, and this angle helps drain excess rainwater from your house to the runoff drain. Incorrectly repairing faulty grading that allows rainwater to gather along your foundation where it can erode soil and potentially cause foundation problems can worsen existing problems. Additionally, it can lead water to neighbouring yards or cause water to pool. Correctly regrading your yard will alleviate drainage problems and keep your home's foundation sound and solid.

Hammer one stake in the yard that needs grading repair 12 inches away from your home and the other stake at the far end of your yard using the rubber mallet. Hammer them to a depth of 18 inches to keep them solidly fixed within the ground.

Tie the twine from stake to sake, keeping it taut.

Spray paint three "depth marks" on the twine at ¼, ½ and ¾ intervals using the orange spray paint.

Calculate your "finished depth grade," knowing that for proper rainwater drainage, the grade should descend away from your foundation at a decline of 12 inches every 50 feet. If your yard measures 100 feet long then the end stake should equal 24 inches, the ¾ mark will measure 18 inches, the ½-way mark will measure 12 inches and the ¼ depth mark will measure 6 inches.

Till the entire yard with the tiller. Tilling loosens the soil, so you can grade it evenly without the tractor's grading blade tearing up large tracts of turf.

Grade the soil in one pass from the house to the first depth mark using the tractor fitted with the grading blade.

Measure the depth between the twine at the ¼ depth mark and the soil, making sure it equals 25 per cent of the finished depth grade. For instance, if your final depth grade equals 100 feet, the space between the twine and the top of the soil should measure 6 inches because at 100 feet, the final depth grade should equal 24 inches and 6 inches equals 25 per cent of 24.

Regrade the ¼ depth mark section of the yard as necessary until you reach the desired depth using the tractor fitted with the grading blade.

Grade the ½ depth mark section until you reach the desired depth.

Grade the rest of the yard, section by section, until you have graded the yard to the finished depth mark.

Stand 10 yards away from the twine, noticing the smoothness of the decline from the house to the final depth mark.

Rake uneven spots as necessary until the entire yard declines away from the house at a depth of 12 inches per 50 feet.

Reseed the yard with grass seed at a rate of 4 to 6 gallons per 100 square feet. Cover the reseeded yard with straw.

Installing French Drains for Yard Drainage

If your neighbour's land stands at a higher elevation than yours, you may be experiencing problems with excessive moisture on your property. Water from your neighbour's property may be running down the slope and spilling onto your property. You need better yard drainage. One option in such cases is installing French drains.

When some people speak of a "French drain", they refer to a trench in which a drain pipe is laid, but the traditional French drain is basically a trench filled with gravel.

Time Required: Depends on extent of water flow and ground to traverse:

1. Determine a spot on your property where the excess water coming off the slope could be re-routed. Determining such a location may end up being a matter of choosing "the lesser of two evils". If water is currently spilling out at your house foundation and excessive moisture threatens to damage it, obviously almost any other spot would be preferable. The ideal French drain leach field would be an out-of-the-way area with sandy soil, through which the water could percolate harmlessly.

2. But be sure your attempt at yard drainage will not adversely impact anyone else's land.Otherwise, installing a French drain could land you a lawsuit! Check your city codes before digging. Another preliminary step that could save you headaches later is checking with your local utilities concerning the whereabouts of underground cables and the like, so that you'll know where not to excavate for a French drain.

3. Locate the best area for a French drain. Find an area along the slope on your side of the boundary where excavation would be easiest for your French drain (i.e., free of obstructions). Trench lines should be plotted out before you begin digging French drains. You need to create your own mini-slope to carry the water down to its destination. A grade of 1 per cent (i.e., a drop of 1 foot for every 100 feet in length) is often recommended for French drains; others advise a drop of 6″ for every 100′. Getting the water to go where you wish is essential for improving yard drainage; the grade will facilitate your efforts.

4. So how do you measure the grading for a French drain? Pound 2 stakes into the ground to mark the beginning and end of the trench. Tie a string tightly to one of the stakes, then run it over to the other stake and tie it off there, too, but loosely (for now). Attach a string level to the string, adjusting the string to get it level. Once it's level, tighten the string at the second stake. Make sure the string is taut. Now begin digging the trench. As you dig, you'll be able to measure down from the string to make sure you are achieving the desired grade for your French drain.

5. Check yourself as you go. For instance, if the trench for the French drain is to be 100′ long and the grade 1 per cent, then by the time your trench is 50′ long, it should be 6″ deeper than where you began excavating.

6. You'll be digging a horizontal trench across the length of the slope. The digging is the most labor-intensive part of installing French drains. The trench will slope down toward the area where you've determined the water will be re-routed (if it doesn't quite reach that spot, you'll have to dig a connecting ditch down to it). Trench width will depend on the magnitude of your moisture problem. Bigger moisture problems call for wider trenches. Small trenches are often dug to a width of 5″-6″.

7. Before applying gravel, line the trench with landscape fabric. The landscape fabric will keep dirt out of the gravel. You want to

preserve the porosity of the gravel, which promotes percolation of water through it—one of the underlying principles that make covered French drains work. Shovel a coarse gravel onto the landscape fabric. Wrap the ends of the landscape fabric over the top of the gravel layer.

8. You now essentially have a tube of landscape fabric filled with gravel. To fill in the rest of the trench, shovel in a layer of coarse sand, cover it with more landscape fabric, add 4" of topsoil and lay sod on top. Your French drain is complete!

Tips

1. Hire a surveyor. If you don't think you can get the grading right for a French drain on your own, hire a surveyor. Or simply hire a pro to do the whole job.
2. Hire a backhoe operator. If you're not inclined to dig a French drain trench by hand, you could hire a backhoe operator. But that will jack up the cost for the French drain—not only for the digging, but for the extra gravel you'll need (since a backhoe can't dig as small a trench as can a person wielding a spade). Another alternative is suggested by reader, Matt Fisher, noting that "many rental shops rent trenchers now. These machines cut very thin trenches...."
3. Bigger not necessarily better. If you can get away with a small trench for your French drain, you'll save money, as there'll be less gravel needed to fill the trench.
4. Terminology. "Gravel" is a term that can be used differently in different regions. Here, "gravel" refers to small pieces of rock.

Things or Instruments that we needed are:

- spade;
- landscape fabric;
- gravel;
- sand;
- sod;
- string level;
- string;
- two stakes; and
- tape measure.

Proper Drainage

Wet basements, flooded yards, and poor plant growth are symptoms of a poorly drained lot. In Iowa, many homes have been built in poorly drained soils. Wet lots generally are caused by ûooding, springs and seeps, seasonal high water tables, ponding of surface water, or slow soil permeability. This publication explains how to deal with these problems and improve the drainage around your home.

Flooding Houses that are in the ûood plains of a nearby stream or creek may be flooded if the stream overflows during periods of heavy rainfall or rapid snow melt.

To avoid areas that might ûood, check with local ofûcials to determine the flood plain boundaries before buying or building a home.

For existing houses in flood plains, determine how you can ensure the safety of occupants and minimize damage from a flood. Be certain that you have an escape route that will be open during a flood. Use dikes, block outlets that might back up into the basement, waterproof the walls, and block windows and doors with sandbags.

During extreme flooding, water pressure can collapse foundation walls. In some cases it might be preferable to allow the basement to flood and equalize water pressure. Contact local authorities to determine the possibility of basement collapse.

Housing developments often modify the landscape and block or alter natural drainage ways. Check site plans carefully before choosing an existing house or purchasing a lot. You may want to ask a housing professional to help you evaluate the adequacy of the drainage on a particular site. Problems in drainage usually require the cooperation of several homeowners.

Springs and Seeps

Natural springs and seeps occur because of existing soil, rock, and landscape characteristics. Water may flow throughout the year or only seasonally during periods of heavy rainfall.

Water may flow into or around your house if it is constructed over or near a spring or seep. Most Iowa houses require subsurface perimeter drains, at least 4 inches in diameter and surrounded with 6 to 12 inches of gravel or sand and gravel, along the outside of the foundation wall. The bottom of the drain tile must be below the basement ûoor, and the tile must slope to an outlet. When possible, drain perimeter drains to a free outlet, storm sewer, or any approved outlet. If none of these options will work, use a sump pump to remove the water.

Springs and seeps also affect lawns and onsite septic ûelds. Install subsurface drains (tile lines) to remove the water. Tile commonly are made of clay, concrete, perforated plastic, metal, asbestos-cement, or bituminous wood ûber. Check with local building codes for approved materials and other drainage regulations.

Seasonal High Water-table

The water table is the upper surface of groundwater. Below the water-table the soil is saturated with water. The level ûuctuates by several feet throughout the year depending on soil, landscape, and weather conditions. In Iowa, the seasonal high water table often is 2 to 5 feet below the ground surface.

In selecting a building site, consider the level of the seasonal high water table. On some sites the seasonal high water table may be at or near the ground surface for long periods. Avoid these areas.

Seasonal high water tables 6-feet deep or more may be of little concern, unless you plan to excavate a deep basement. Subsurface drains such as those used to handle springs and seeps can be used to lower the water table. You'll need a good outlet for the discharge flow and adequate capacity to handle the most severe conditions. Sump pumps should have a back-up power supply in case of power failure.

It is preferable to build the basement ûoor above the seasonal high water table. Provide drainage under the basement ûoor with 4 to 6 inches of free-draining material and a subsurface drainage system. Use a moisture barrier and high quality concrete to reduce water migration through the floor.

Seasonal high water tables around existing houses can be lowered by installing drainage around the outside wall or under the basement floor. Both methods are expensive and disrup tive. Lowering the water table under the basement ûoor should be done with caution. On some soils, especially slow-draining silts and clays, unequal settling may crack the walls.

To remove water from the interior of concrete block walls, install drainage channels at the intersection of the wall and the ûoor. These channels are commercially available.

Ponding of Surface Water

You can use small diversions or ditches to channel water away from your lot. Various regulations concerning water flow will apply and you must not change the flow in a way that adversely affects your neighbour. Before beginning a project, check with your neighbours and local ofûcials.

Surface inlets can be used to carry water to a subsurface drain. The drain outlet can empty into street gutters or storm sewers if permitted by local building codes.

Grade your yard so that surface water drains away from the house. Often the wall used around a house settles, leaving a low area. It must be ûlled so water runs away from the house. In the first 10 feet away from the house, the soil should drop a minimum of 6 inches.

A minimum grade of 1 foot in 100 feet is generally adequate after the first 10 feet.

To prevent wood rot, the soil around a house must not be too close to the wood siding. There must be at least 8 inches between the soil and the wood siding. The soil directly around the house should be of slow permeability so water does not penetrate near the house. Do not use rock and gravel on the surface, since they will serve as a conduit for water into the ground.

Avoid using the same subsurface drain for perimeter tile around the foundation and for the downspout. If the capacity of the drain is not sufficient, excess water will be dumped around the basement footings.

Water from downspouts that empty onto the lawn must be dumped and spread far enough from the house so the water does not enter the basement. On steeply sloping well-drained lawns with no basement water problems, a simple splash block usually will be Sufficient. For houses with basement water problems, the water should be dumped at least 5 to 10 feet from the house.

Slow Soil Permeability

Dense layers of soil will restrict the flow of water, and water may pond on the lawn. If the problem is due to poor drainage through the soil, you can drain small wet areas by digging a small trench through the layer and filling it with sand or gravel to improve permeability. However, this method will not work if the problem is caused by a high water table.

Drain larger wet areas by installing subsurface drains 4 to 6 inches in diameter at a depth of 2 to 5 feet. The drains should be back-filled to within a foot of the ground surface with sand or gravel. Use porous topsoil to fill the last foot.

How to Grade a Lawn for Drainage

Lawn grading around your house should take runoff water away from the foundation. If the soil grading drains water toward your house instead, you can end up with a wet basement or cracks around your foundation.

While most contractors include landscape grading when they finish a new building, older homes often need to have the ground worked so it drains properly. You can do it yourself if you understand the basic principles. In all likelihood, your grass is going to need replanting when you finish the project.

Determine the slope of the land so you know how much lawn grading is necessary. Ideally, you need 1 foot of drop for every 50 feet away from your foundation. Attach one end of a 50-foot length of string to a stake and place the stake in the ground near the foundation of the house. Tie the other end to a second stake and place that stake 50 feet from the house. Use a level to level the string. You may need to do this in several locations around the perimeter of your house.

Use a tape measure to determine how high the string is from the ground at the 50-foot mark. If it's one feet, the slope is just right. If it's less than 12 inches, you should consider adding more slope to your yard. The difference is how much soil you need to grade off the lawn. If it measures more than 12 inches, you have more than adequate slope.

Rent a skid-steer tractor with front loader to move the dirt. Remove 6 to 8 inches of topsoil from the area where you are adding more lawn drainage. Place the topsoil in a pile. Remove the subsoil and put it in a separate pile. Once you remove enough subsoil, replace the topsoil and smooth the surface slope. If you only need to adjust the slope for a small portion of your yard, you may be able to do it by hand with a shovel.

Build up low areas by removing the topsoil. Put the subsoil you removed earlier in the low spots. Cover them with topsoil.

Clean up any rocks, roots or other debris on the ground's surface. Use a rake to smooth the surface of the ground. Flip the rake over and use its back to smooth the surface even more.

Maps and Records

A map is a visual representation of an area—a symbolic depiction highlighting relationships between elements of that space such as objects, regions, and themes.

Many maps are static two-dimensional, geometrically accurate (or approximately accurate) representations of three-dimensional space, while others are dynamic or interactive, even three-dimensional. Although most commonly used to depict geography, maps may represent any space, real or imagined, without regard to context or scale; e.g. Brain mapping, DNA mapping, and extra terrestrial mapping.

PRESERVING AGRICULTURAL RECORDS

Why should we be interested in identifying and preserving agricultural records? They are a means by which our culture is passed from one generation to the next, and they provide information from which one generation can learn from its predecessors. Today, there is more interest in family and community history, a need to understand one's "roots". People can learn much about their ancestors, the first immigrants who came to Orange County to reclaim the black dirt from the undrained bogs. Many different ethnic groups were involved with farming in this area.

Agricultural records are indispensable sources for the work of historians and other specialists who interpret the past for present and future use. Many agricultural records have immediate, practical, everyday uses. They are of use to government officials, public interest groups, and to business people. They provide information essential for research into environmental, health and welfare issues, and farming trends.

Agricultural records can be used in the classroom to help students better understand the lives of farmers, the machinery they used, the crops that were planted, the organizations to which they belonged to protect their interests. Younger generations and scholars can use the records to learn about the culture and their ancestors through the use of such records.

By identifying, collecting and preserving farming records now, future generations will have a better understanding of farmers' lives in the present and the past. These records are an important part of Orange County History as well as New York State History.

PRACTICE OF CARTOGRAPHY

Cartography or map-making is the study and practice of crafting representations of the Earth upon a flat surface, and one who makes maps is called a cartographer.

Road maps are perhaps the most widely used maps today, and form a subset of navigational maps, which also include aeronautical and nautical charts, railroad network maps, and hiking and bicycling maps. In terms of quantity, the largest number of drawn map sheets is probably made up by local surveys, carried out by municipalities, utilities, tax assessors, emergency services providers, and other local agencies. Many national surveying projects have been carried out by the military, such as the British Ordnance Survey now a civilian government agency internationally renowned for its comprehensively detailed work.

In addition to location information maps may also be used to portray contour lines (isolines) indicating constant values of elevation, temperature, rainfall, etc.

Orientation of Maps

The orientation of a map is the relationship between the directions on the map and the corresponding compass directions in reality. The word "orient" is derived from Latin oriens, meaning East. In the Middle Ages many maps, including the T and O maps, were drawn with East at the top (meaning that the direction "up" on the map corresponds to East on the compass). Today, the most common – but far from universal – cartographic convention is that North is at the top of a map. Several kinds of maps are often traditionally not oriented with North at the top:

- Maps from non-Western traditions are oriented a variety of ways. Old maps of Edo show the Japanese imperial palace as the "top", but also at the centre, of the map. Labels on the map are oriented in such a way that you cannot read them properly unless you put the imperial palace above your head.

- Medieval European T and O maps such as the Hereford Mappa Mundi were centred on Jerusalem with East at the top. Indeed, prior to the reintroduction of Ptolemy's Geography to Europe around 1400, there was no single convention in the West. Portolan charts, for example, are oriented to the shores they describe.
- Maps of cities bordering a sea are often conventionally oriented with the sea at the top.
- Route and channel maps have traditionally been oriented to the road or waterway they describe.
- Polar maps of the Arctic or Antarctic regions are conventionally centred on the pole; the direction North would be towards or away from the centre of the map, respectively. Typical maps of the Arctic have 0° meridian towards the bottom of the page; maps of the Antarctic have the 0° meridian towards the top of the page.
- Reversed maps, also known as Upside-Down maps or South-Up maps, reverse the "North is up" convention and have South at the top.
- Buckminster Fuller's Dymaxion maps are based on a projection of the Earth's sphere onto anicosahe dron. The resulting triangular pieces may be arranged in any order or orientation.
- Modern digital GIS maps such as ArcMap typically project north at the top of the map, but use math degrees (0 is east, degrees increase counter-clockwise), rather than compass degrees (0 is north, degrees increase clockwise) for orientation of transects. Compass decimal degrees can be converted to math degrees by subtracting them from 450.

Map Types and Projections

Maps of the world or large areas are often either 'political' or 'physical'. The most important purpose of the political map is to show territorial borders; the purpose of the physical is to show features of geography such as mountains, soil type or land use including infrastruction such as roads, railroads and buildings.Topographic maps show elevations and relief with contour linesor shading. Geological maps show not only the physical surface, but characteristics of the underlying rock, fault lines, and subsurface structures.

Maps that depict the surface of the Earth also use a projection, a way of translating the three-dimensional real surface of the geoid to a two-dimensional picture. Perhaps the best-known world-map projection is the Mercator projection, originally designed as a form of nautical chart.

Aeroplane pilots use aeronautical charts based on a Lambert conformal conic projection, in which a cone is laid over the section of the earth to be mapped. The cone intersects the sphere (the earth) at one or two parallels which are chosen as standard lines. This allows the pilots to plot a great-circle route approximation on a flat, two-dimensional chart.

- Azimuthal or Gnomonic map projections are often used in planning air routes due to their ability to represent great circles as straight lines.
- Richard Edes Harrison produced a striking series of maps during and after World War II for Fortune magazine. These used "bird's eye" projections to emphasise globally strategic "fronts" in the air age, pointing out proximities and barriers not apparent on a conventional rectangular projection of the world.

Electronic Maps

From the last quarter of the 20th century, the indispensable tool of the cartographer has been the computer. Much of cartography, especially at the data-gathering survey level, has been subsumed by Geographic Information Systems (GIS). The functionality of maps has been greatly advanced by technology simplifying the superimposition of spatially located variables onto existing geographical maps. Having local information such as rainfall level, distribution of wildlife, or demographic data integrated within the map allows more efficient analysis and better decision making. In the pre-electronic age such superimposition of data led Dr. John Snowto discover the cause of cholera. Today, it is used by agencies of the human kind, as diverse as wildlife conservationists and agricultarists around the world.

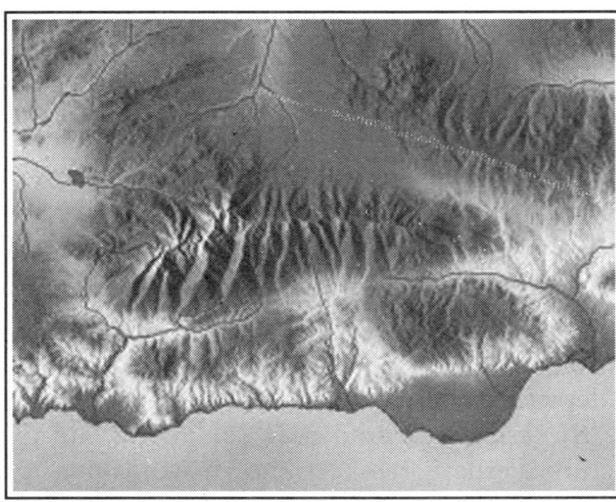

Fig. 7.1: Relief map Sierra Nevada

Even when GIS is not involved, most cartographers now use a variety of computer graphics programmes to generate new maps.

Interactive, computerised maps are commercially available, allowing users to zoom in or zoom out (respectively eaning to increase or decrease the scale), sometimes by replacing one map with another of different scale, centered where possible on the same point. In-car global navigation satellite systems are computerised maps with route-planning and advice facilities which monitor the user's position with the help of satellites. From the computer scientist's point of view, zooming in entails one or a combination of:

1. Replacing the map by a more detailed one
2. Enlarging the same map without enlarging the pixels, hence showing more detail by removing less information compared to the less detailed version
3. Enlarging the same map with the pixels enlarged (replaced by rectangles of pixels); no additional detail is shown, but, depending on the quality of one's vision, possibly more detail can be seen; if a computer display does not show adjacent pixels really separate, but overlapping instead (this does not apply for an LCD, but may apply for a cathode ray tube), then replacing a picture by a rectangle of picture does show more detail. A variation of this method is interpolation.

Agricultural crops of Black Dirt Region

The black dirt region, originally called "the drowned lands", consists of the remains of a great shallow lake, which formed as the last glaciers were melting away 12,000 years ago. As the ice continued to retreat, the climate warmed and lush vegetation grew, died, and sank to the bottom of the lake. Eventually, most of the lake became swampy, and the decaying organic matter continued to accumulate in the water to a depth in excess of twelve feet in places. The shallow lake lay in this valley from that time until about 100 years ago, when immigrants came to this area and realized the value of the soil which lay below what they then called "the drowned lands".

Orange County produces one half the onions grown in New York State on 5500 acres in the black dirt area. The main type of onion grown is the yellow globe, which is a premium cooking onion. Black dirt onions have been shipped as far away as Israel, and also to the northeastern states and southern state markets. Once known as the "Onion Capital of the United States", the black dirt farmers now face competition from areas having longer growing seasons. Other crops grown in the black dirt area include lettuce, radishes, cabbage, carrots, corn, pumpkin, squash, and there are also sod farms.

Site and Survey Participants

The following list of organizations, farmers, historical societies, and businesses were contacted for the purpose of creating this resource guide. Participants listed in bold print make up this finding aid due to the fact that a substantial amount of both historical and archival material relating to agriculture in the black dirt region were located at those sites. It should be noted, however, that other listed survey participants might also hold similar records but did not participate in the initial or secondary survey.

8 Grading the Ditches for Tile

It is exactly so with the question of the cost of drainage. If the work is insecurely done, and is liable, in five years or in fifty, to become worthless; the increase of the crops resulting from it, must not only cover the yearly interest on the cost, but the yearly depreciation as well. Therefore what may seem at the time of doing the work to be cheapness, is really the greatest extravagance. It is like building a brick wall with clay for mortar.

The bricks and the workmanship cost full price, and the small saving on the mortar will topple the wall over in a few years, while, if well cemented, it would have lasted for centuries. The cutting and filling of the ditches, and the purchase and transportation of the tiles, will cost the same in every case, and these constitute the chief cost; if the proper care in grading, tile-laying and covering, and in making outlets be stingily withheld—saving, perhaps, one-tenth of the expense—what might have been a permanent improvement to the land, may disappear, and the whole outlay be lost in ten years. A saving of ten per cent. in the cost will have lost us the other ninety in a short time.

But, while cheapness is to be shunned, economy is to be sought in every item of the work of draining, and should be studied, by proprietor and engineer, from the first examination of the land, to the throwing of the last shovelful of earth on to the filling of the ditch. There are few operations connected with the cultivation of the soil in which so much may be imperceptibly lost through neglect, and carelessness about little details, as in tile-draining.

In the original levelling of the ground, the adjustment of the lines, the establishing of the most judicious depth and inclination at each point of the drains, the disposition of surface streams during the prosecution of the work, and in the width of the excavation, the line which divides economy and wastefulness is extremely narrow and the most constant vigilance, together with the best judgment and foresight, are needed to avoid unnecessary cost.

In the laying and covering of the tile, on the other hand, it is best to disregard a little slowness and unnecessary care on the part of the workmen, for the sake of the most perfect security of the work.

Costing and Expenditure

The items of the work of drainage may be classified as follows:

It is not easy to say what would be the proper charge for this item of the work. In England, the Commissioners under the Drainage Acts of Parliament, and the Boards of Public Works, fix the charge for engineering at $1.25 per acre. That is in a country when the extent of lands undergoing the process of draining is very great, enabling one person to superintend large tracts in the same neighborhood at the same time, and with little or no outlay for travelling expenses. In this country, where the improvement is, thus far, confined to small areas, widely separated; and where there are comparatively few engineers who make a specialty of the work, the charge for services is necessarily much higher, and the amount expended in travelling much greater. In most cases, the proprietor of the land must qualify himself to superintend his own operations, (with the aid of a country surveyor, or a railroad engineer in the necessary instrumental work.) As draining becomes more general, the demand for professional assistance will, without doubt, cause local engineers to turn their attention to the subject, and their services may be more cheaply obtained. At present, it would probably not be prudent to estimate the cost of engineering and superintendence, including the time and skill of the proprietor, at less than $5 per acre, even where from 20 to 50 acres are to be drained at once.

The effect of the silt-basin is to retard the flow of the water, and hence should never be used where this will prove injurious to the drains. The breaking of the current and the entrance friction of the outlet pipe, while it causes the silt to be deposited, also diminishes the velocity and discharge of the main drain, and is detrimental to the action of the drain on level grades.

Where there is abundant fall and the entering drains can discharge into the basin not less than one foot above the top of the outlet drain it may be used.

The best plan for collecting the water of several drains into one is by means of the Y junction and a * 'drop' from branch into main as noted heretofore. The current is preserved, and silt is carried to the outlet before it is deposited. Where the drains are well laid completely graded ditch at the rate of from 10 to 20 rods per hour.

It is governed and operated in the same manner as a traction engine, is compactly built and easily managed by two men. It cannot be expected that a machine of this character will work successfully in ground so soft that it will not bear the weight of the machine, nor in land full of stumps, stones, and large roots. With these exceptions, there seem to be no difficulties which are not successfully met by this machine.

Contracts of Drains

The construction of drains for improving entire farms and large areas of level land is frequently done by contract subject to competent superintendence. The system is laid out by an engineer and complete plans made for the work, after which bids for the construction of the drains are solicited. The furnishing of the tile and distribution as needed upon the ground is usually not included in the ditching contract, neither is the filling of the trenches.

Tile are purchased by the thousand feet; hauling from the railroad station or factory is done by the ton, the weight of the individual pieces of different sizes being used as a basis for determining the weight of the loads ; the digging of ditches and laying of tile is commonly done by the rod, but by the 100 feet would be better, and filling of the ditches by the 100 feet.

The following general specifications and contract have been found useful in practice, and will serve as a guide in preparing specifications for other work. It will be observed that the only bond or security required of the contractor is the 25 per cent retained until the completion and acceptance of the work. The only method of securing good work of this kind is to give it thorough supervision and know that it is right before the drain is covered.

When a drain has been accepted the liability of the contractor should cease provided the individual line has been finished. The retaining of 25 per cent is made for the purpose of securing the correction of any faults in the work which may be discovered before the drain is covered.

SPECIFICATIONS FOR THE CONSTRUCTION OF TILE DRAINS

The lines for the ditches are indicated on the field by stakes which have been set by the engineer, and the depths and grades given by him shall constitute a part of these specifications.

Digging the Ditches

The digging of each ditch must begin at its outlet, or at its junction with another tile drain, arrd proceed toward its upper end. The ditch must be dug along one side of the line of survey stakes, and about ten inches distant from it, in a straight and neat manner, and the top soil thrown on one side of the ditch and the clay on the other.

When a change in the direction of ditch is made, it must be done by means of a neat curve, but in all cases the ditch must be kept near enough to the stakes so that they can be used in grading the bottom. In taking out the last draft, the blade of the spade must not go deeper thr.n the proposed grade line or bed upon which the tiles are to rest.

Grading the Bottom

The ditch must be dug to the depth indicated by the figures given with the survey, which depth is to be measured from the grade stakes which are set for that purpose, and graded evenly on the bottom by means of the "line and gauge" method, or "target", or any other equally accurate device for obtaining an even and true bottom upon which to lay the tile. The bottom must be dressed with the tile hoe, or in case of large tiles, with the shovel, so that a groove will be made to receive the tile, and when laid in it they will remain securely in place.

Laying the Tile

The laying of the tile must begin at the lower end and proceed up-stream. The tile must be laid as closely as practicable, and in lines free from irregular crooks, the pieces being turned about until the upper edge closes, unless there is sand or fine silt which is likely to run into the tile, in which case the lower edge must be laid close, and the upper side covered with clay or other suitable material. When, in making turns, or by reason of irregular-shaped tile, a crack of one fourth inch or more is necessarily left, it must be securely covered with broken pieces of tile. Junctions with branch lines must be carefully and securely made.

Blinding the Tile

After the tile have been laid and inspected by the person in charge of the work, they must be covered with clay to a depth of six inches, unless, in the judgment of the superintendent, the tile are sufficiently firm, so that complete filling of the ditch may be made directly upon the tile. In no case must the tile be covered with sand without other material being first used.

Risk During Construction

The ditch contractor must assume all risks from storms and caving in of ditches, and when each drain is completed it must be free from sand and mud before it will be received and paid for in full. In case it is found impracticable, by reason of bad weather or unlooked-for trouble in digging the ditch, or properly laying the tile, to complete the work at the time specified in the contract, the time may be extended as may be mutually agreed upon by employer and contractor. The contractor shall use all necessary precaution to secure his work from injury while he is constructing the drain.

Tile to be Used

Tile will be delivered on the ground convenient for the use of the contractor. No tile must be laid which are broken, or soft, or so badly out of shape that they cannot be well laid and make a good and satisfactory drain.

Payments for Work

Unless otherwise hereafter agreed upon, the contractor may at any time claim and receive from the employer seventy-five per cent of the value of completed and accepted work at the price agreed upon in the contract. Twenty-five per cent will be retained until the entire work contracted for is completed and accepted, at which time the whole ount due will be paid.

Prosecution of the Work

The work must be pushed as fast as will be onsistent with economy and good workman-ship and must not be left by the contractor for the purpose of working upon other contracts, except by permission and consent of the employer.

Digging Tile Ditches with Machines

Many machines of different patterns have been patented, tried, and have failed to displace hand labor in digging tile ditches. The difficulties to overcome do not seem insurmountable, nevertheless the history of such machines discloses partial successes which for a time promised well, but in the end did not meet the requirements of the work in all kinds and conditions of soils. Ploughs of different patterns have been used to aid the spade by loosening the earth in the bottom of the ditch, thereby diminishing the labor of excavating somewhat.

The machines which have dug the ditch to its full depth at one passage have given the most satisfactory results. The ditch is left completed to grade and ready for the laying of the tile, the excavated earth is left loose and ready to be easily backfilled and the grade is more easily and accurately made than by a machine which excavates by many passages over the ground.

One of these machines which gives excellent results at the present writing and has been more successfully introduced than its predecessors is distinctively a traction ditcher. It is propelled by steam power which operates a cutting wheel and at the same time moves the machine forward by traction, excavating a completely graded ditch at the rate of from 10 to 20 rods per hour. It is governed and operated in the same manner as a traction engine, is compactly built and easily managed by two men. It cannot be expected that a machine of this character will work succcessfully in ground so soft that it will not bear the weight of the machine, nor in land full of stumps, stones, and large roots.

The construction of drains for improving entire farms and large areas of level land is frequently done by contract subject to competent superintendence. The system is laid out by an engineer and complete plans made for the work, after which bids for the construction of the drains are solicited. The furnishing of the tile and distribution as needed upon the ground is usually not included in the ditching contract, neither is the filling of the trenches.

Tile are purchased by the thousand feet; hauling from the railroad station or factory is done by the ton, the weight of the individual pieces of different sizes being used as a basis for determining the weight of the loads ; the digging of ditches and laying of tile is commonly done by the rod, but by the 100 feet would be better, and filling of the ditches by the 100 feet.

The following general specifications and contract have been found useful in practice, and will serve as a guide in preparing specifications for other work. It will be observed that the only bond or security required of the contractor is the 25 per cent retained until the completion and acceptance of the work. The only method of securing good work of this kind is to give it thorough supervision and know that it is right before the drain is covered.

When a drain has been accepted the liability of the contractor should cease provided the individual line has been finished. The retaining of 25 per cent is made for the purpose of securing the correction of any faults in the work which may be discovered before the drain is covered.

Types of Tile

The term "ceramic tile" is a rather loose one, inasmuch as a number of tiling and paving products are included in the description. Ceramic wall tiles made from "slip," the same material figurines are made from; monocottura (single-fired) floor tiles; rock-hard porcelain tiles; and mosaic tiles made from either porcelain or clay are some of the varieties called "ceramic tiles".

Wall Tiles

A wall tile is any tile used primarily in applications other than floors. The most prevalent of these are "standard American wall tiles," which also go by the term "four-and-a-quarter," since they are approximately 4¼ inches square.

Four-and-a-quarter tiles are those which have been used in bathrooms since the advent of inside plumbing in this country. Many companies make them, and thus there are myriad colours and textures available. Trim pieces or "shapes" are available for every style of standard wall tile made. This is important when it comes to building showers and other structures that require outside corners and edges.

Four-and-a-quarter tiles are almost always formed from "slip", the white ceramic clay used in figurines. The tiles are water-resistant but not water-proof.

There are a number of porcelain tiles which are also designed to be used on walls and surfaces other than floors. Most of these are glazed, and many of them are made in other countries, particularly Asian countries including Japan and Korea. Many times these tiles arrive mounted on backing sheets which facilitate their installation. Porcelain tiles, glazed or unglazed, are virtually water-proof.

Tiles used at the waterlines of swimming pools are usually glazed porcelain tiles. These are almost always imported from other countries, most notably Japan.

Floor Tiles (glazed)

Almost all the glazed floor tiles used today are single-fired "monocottura" tiles. They are made by the process known as "dust pressing", wherein very little water is used, and the bisques or tile bodies are compacted under extremely high pressure.

Glazing is then accomplished, and the tile is cooked at high temperatures, usually over 2000 degrees. A tile produced in this manner is very durable and will last indefinitely.

Grading

In the United States there are five grades assigned to floor tiles, whether they are imported or produced in this country. The grades are in Roman numerals, with grade I being the lowest and V the highest. I know of no one who makes grade I tiles however, so let's start with II.

Grade II tiles can be used in residential applications where light traffic is expected. Bathroom floors, for example, do not receive very heavy traffic.

Grade III tiles are adequate for any residential use, including kitchen and entry floors, which receive considerable traffic. These tiles might also be used in light-traffic commercial applications — perhaps beauty parlors and other businesses where there is not a heavy and continuous volume of foot traffic..

Grade IV tiles are rated commercial, although they are also commonly used in homes. These tiles will hold up in just about any application, including grocery stores, bank lobbies, etc.

Grade V tiles are used in industrial settings, where they are expected to receive heavy abuse and exposure to various chemicals. Not many grade V tiles would be used in the home. They usually look too commercial.

Tile grades are never stamped on packaging, so you are at the mercy of the person selling you the tile. This is one of the reasons we suggest you do your shopping at established tile supply locations and not at discount stores and home centers. Only people who specialize in a product are going to know a great deal about it. Home center employees, for example, simply have too many products to keep up with.

Quarry Tiles

Quarry tiles are made from the same clay bricks are made of. Quarry tiles, including brick pavers, paving bricks and paving tiles are all from the family known as "burnt clay." These tiles come in different sizes and shapes: some are square, some are irregular, and some are generally shaped like bricks laid flat — about four by eight inches or so.

All of the burnt clay materials are extremely durable, inasmuch as they are fired hard, and the color pigments go all the way through from top to bottom. They are rated at grade IV or V. Quarry tiles will never wear out no matter how much abuse they're subjected to.

Porcelain Floor Tiles

Porcelain tiles are probably the hardest products we install. They are dense to the point that they are water-proof, and they are extremely difficult to cut. We wear out more cutting tools on porcelain tiles than on any other product.

Unglazed porcelains are often used in commercial and industrial applications. During manufacturing they can be given non-slip surfaces which make them desirable in outdoor settings and in other instances where the tiles can be expected to become wet. I installed unglazed porcelain tiles in bank lobbies for years—all over Texas, as well as in Louisiana, Arkansas, and Mississippi.

Recently we have encountered more and more glazed porcelain tiles, which are wonderful for residential use. The glaze gives them a warmer look than the unglazed versions. These tiles are generally more expensive than their clay counterparts, though.

Almost all floor tiles used in the U.S. and Canada nowadays are made from porcelain. I don't expect the trend to change. Porcelain tiles have a water absorption rate of .5 or less. There are tiles labeled porcelain that do not meet the absorption standard. If you have any doubt, ask to see the product data. If none are available, move on.

Mosaic Tiles

Mosaics are any tiles, glazed or unglazed, that measure 2 inches square or less, although they don't necessarily have to be square. Some of them, in fact, are hexagonal in shape and others are rectangles. It doesn't matter what the tiles are made of, however most mosaics are made from porcelain, and most of them are left unglazed.

Mosaic tiles are used extensively in commercial applications. Walk into a commercial restroom, and you'll probably notice porcelain mosaic tiles on the floor and possibly on the walls as well.

We often use mosaics to form residential shower floors. The small size makes it feasible to "dish" the shower floor so that water readily flows toward the drain. It is almost impossible to accomplish this with larger pieces and make the job look good. The numerous grout joints between the small tiles provide a great deal of "tooth," and this translates to slip resistance on bare feet.

Mosaic tiles are always mounted on sheets of backing paper or netting—or they are joined together with small spots of synthetic rubber. It has been at least fifty years since they were delivered and installed individually. Can you imagine the time that took?

There are also natural clay tiles, including terracotta tiles and Saltillo tiles. Terracotta tiles are the color of the clay from which they are produced, ranging from grays to browns and reddish orange. They are left unglazed and require a top finish after installation. Saltillo tiles are covered in another article.

An important consideration for all tiles installed outdoors is whether the tiles are "frost-proof." This is especially true in northern climes where freezing conditions are commonplace. Generally, the degree of frost resistance in a tile is determined by its propensity to absorb water. In this sense, tiles that are water-proof are also frost-proof.

Since water expands when it freezes, if it is allowed to get in or under tiles in freezing conditions, it can cause the tiles to crack and come loose. Many ceramic floor tiles, porcelain tiles and all quarry tiles are safe bets for outdoor applications. Terracottas and other natural clay tiles, including Saltillo tiles should not be used in areas where hard freezes occur.

Grade Italian Porcelain Tile

Tile is rated based on a grading system from 1 to 5, with 1 being the lowest or weakest grade of tile and 5 being the highest or strongest and most durable grade. This rating system is used in the United States for both tiles manufactured in the US and tiles imported from other countries. The grade of the tile is not stamped on the tile, so to determine the grade you will need to ask the tile manufacturer or store where the tile is purchased. Italian porcelain tile falls under this grading system as well.

Determine the grade of tile that you need for your project. Grade I tile is typically used for walls because it is so weak. Grade II tile can be used for floors in areas that do not have heavy foot traffic. Grade III tiles are often used in residential buildings for tile floors, counter tops and other areas that do not receive a great amount of use. Grade IV tiles are commonly used in residential buildings as well as offices and commercial buildings and are very durable. Grade V tiles are the strongest tiles and are used in high traffic commercial areas.

Locate a home improvement store or tile store. Shop for and pick out an Italian porcelain tile that will fit your project.

Locate a sales representative or store manager and ask them for the grade of the tile. If the sales representative or manager does not have access to the tile-grading information, write down the name of the tile manufacturer.

Contact the tile manufacturer. Request the manufacturer's contact information from the tile retailer or use an Internet search engine to locate the contact information. For any query clarification, it is advisable to contact the tile grade information from the manufacturing company.

9 Flow of Water Through Pipes

To understand the operating principles of an electronic drive and motor, it is necessary to understand the basic principles of electricity.

Electricity comes in two forms: alternating current (AC) and direct current (DC). We will first consider the effects of DC on various electrical components and identify the three main characteristics of any electrical circuit.

When we take a close look at nature, we find all matter is composed of atoms. In the basic structure of an atom, we find the nucleus is at the center, surrounded by one or more orbiting electrons. This structure re-occurs millions of times for any material. If the material is an insulator, the orbiting electrons do not move from place to place or from atom to atom. For the purposes of discussion, we will consider a conductor as an atom with three or less orbiting electrons in the outer shell. An atom with five or more orbiting electrons will be an insulator.

Electrons in the outer orbiting rings find it easy to move from atom to atom (particularly in a conductor like a copper wire) whenever they are forced to do so. The force that tends to move electrons is voltage (electrical pressure in a circuit). Voltage is basically the force that causes electrons to travel from atom to atom.

As you would expect, the higher the voltage, the more force available to move electrons. Some textbooks use the term electromotive force when describing voltage. Electrons move from atom to atom to take up a spot vacated by the previous electron. Electrons flow in an orderly manner through a conductor.

Completing the Circuit

A typical comparison is to water flow in a pipe with that of electron flow in a conductor. When you turn on a water faucet, a certain amount of water pressure forces water through the pipe and out the end of the faucet. The exact same phenomena holds true for electricity. When you turn on a light, you allow voltage (force) to push electrons (current) through the wire and cause the light to illuminate.

The movement of electrons in a conductor

Electrons move to a vacant spot

Voltage

Conductor

Water flow in a pipe vs. electron flow in a conductor

Water Pressure

Pressure forcing water through a pipe

Voltage

Voltage forcing electrons through a pipe

Energy comes from the pump and the battery. It travels to the load (the water fountain and the light bulb). At the load, energy manifests as moving water and light/heat

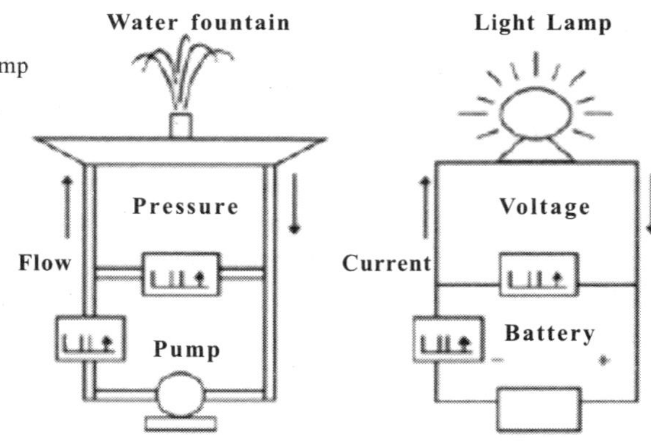

Fig. 9.1

The obvious question is why is it necessary to move electrons in the first place? The reason is fundamental: Every electrical user (light bulb, TV, toaster, a motor) has resistance, measured in ohms. The user of electricity is an electrical load. A simple fluid circuit consists of a pump to supply the source of water pressure. The water fountain is the load. The pipes provide the path for the water to flow and also provide a certain amount of resistance to flow. A simple electrical circuit consists of a source of electrons (battery), a load (light bulb), and conductors (wires) to complete the circuit.

Flow of Water Through Pipes Formulas

Velocity of Flow

When water flows through a pipe of uniform cross section, the quantity of water passing any point in a given interval of time depends upon the velocity with which the water flows and the area of cross section of the pipe. It is evident that the quantity of water will equal a column whose cross section is the area of the pipe and whose length is equal to the velocity.

The velocity with which water moves through a pipe is not uniform throughout its cross section. It is least near the wetted perimeter of the pipe where the friction of the pipe retards the flow, and is greatest at the center of the cross section where having to overcome only the friction of its own flowing layers, it attains the maximum velocity. It is assumed in practice, however, that all particles of the water have the same velocity, and the mean of all the velocities in the cross section is taken as the velocity of flow.

Formulas for Velocity

When the size of a pipe and the quantity of water it will discharge in a given time are known, the mean velocity of efflux can be found by the formula: v=q.a.

In which

v = velocity of flow in feet per minute q = quantity of water in cubic feet per minute

a = area of cross section of pipe in square feet.*

Example

What must be the velocity of flow in a 2-inch pipe to discharge 6.3 cubic feet of water per minute ?

Solution

Area of pipe = .0213 square feet. Then 6.3/.0213 - 300 feet per minute.

When the hydrostatic head, length and diameter of a pipe are known, the mean velocity of discharge can be found by the formula:

$$V = m\sqrt{\frac{hd}{1+54d}}$$

In which V = mean velocity in feet per second m = coefficient from Table 9.1 = diameter of pipe in feet h = hydrostatic head in feet i = total length of pipe in feet

Table 9.1: Values of Coefficient

$V = m\sqrt{\frac{hd}{1+54d}}$	Diameter of Pipe in							
	Feet	**Feet**	**Feet**	**Feet**	**Feet**	**Feet**	**Feet**	**Feet**
	.05	.10	.50	1	1.5	2	3	4
	Ins	Ins.	Ins.	Ins.	Ins.	Ins.	Ins.	Ins.
	5/8	11/4	6	12	18	24	36	48
	m	m	m	m	m	m	m	m
.005	29	31	33	35	37	40	44	47
.01	34	35	37	39	42	45	49	53
.02	39	40	42	45	49	52	56	59
.03	41	43	47	50	54	57	60	63
.05	44	47	52	54	56	60	64	67
.10	47	50	54	56	58	62	66	70
.20	48	51	55	58	60	64	67	70

Example

What will be the velocity of discharge from a 6-inch pipe 500 feet long under a head of 60 feet?

Table of square inches in decimals of a square foot in appendix.

Solution

$$V = 55\sqrt{\frac{60 \times .5}{500 + (54 \times .5)}}$$

$$= 55\sqrt{\frac{80}{527}}$$

$$= 55\sqrt{0.567} = 55 \times .298 = 18.09 \text{ feet per second}$$

In column 1 of Table 9.1 will be found that the nearest value corresponding to .238 is .20, and following that line to where it intersects the column headed 6 inches, the value of coefficient m will be found to be 55, which multiplied by the square root .238 gives the velocity sought for. Where great accuracy of calculation is not required, the constant 48, which is an average value of coefficients for small sizes of pipes, can be used, and will give results sufficiently accurate for most practical purposes.

Formula for Head

When the length and diameter of a pipe are known, the head required to discharge a certain quantity of water per second can be found by the formula:

h=.000704q21

In which h=head in feet l=length of pipe in feet d=diameter of pipe in feet q=quantity of water in cubic feet per second.

Example

What head will be required to discharge from a 4-inch pipe 500 feet long 2 cubic feet of water per second ?

Solution

Substituting values in the formula $h = 0.000704 \times 4 \times 500 = 333$ feet head.

$= 0.00422$

Formula for Diameter

When the length of a pipe, the hydrostatic head, and the quantity of water required to be delivered per second are. known, the diameter of pipe that will safely take care of that quantity can be found by the formula:

$$d = .234\sqrt[5]{\frac{q^2 1}{h}}$$

In which d=diameter of pipe in feet q=cubic feet per second to be delivered l=length of pipe in feet h=head in feet.

Example - What diameter of pipe will be required to deliver .5 cubic foot of water per second through a pipe 2,000 feet long with a head of 400 feet?

Solution

$$-d = .234\sqrt[5]{\frac{.25 \times 2.000}{400}}$$

$$= .245 \text{ feet} = 3 \text{ inch pipe}$$

Formulas for Quantity

When the mean velocity and the area of a pipe are known, the quantity of water discharged in a given interval of time can be determined by the formula:

$$q = va$$

In which q=quantity of water in cubic feet per minute v=velocity of flow in feet per minute a=area of cross section of pipe in square feet

Example

How many cubic feet of water will be discharged per minute by a 2-inch pipe when the velocity of efflux is 300 feet per minute?

Solution

Area of 2-inch pipe=.021 square feet. Then .021 × 300 =6.3 cubic feet. Answer.

When the diameter, head and length of a pipe are known, the quantity of water it will deliver in a given time can be found by the formula:

$$q = \sqrt{\frac{d^2h}{1}} \times 4.71$$

In which q=quantity in cubic feet per minute d=diameter of pipe in inches h=head in feet l=length of pipe in feet

Example

What quantity of water can be delivered per minute through a 3-inch pipe 2,000 feet long with a head of 400 feet?

Solution

$$-q = \sqrt{\frac{243 \times 400}{2,000}} \times 4.71$$

$$= 32.97 \text{ cubic feet pe minute}$$

The velocity of flow in drains or pipes running partly full can be found by the formula:

$$V = \sqrt{\frac{a}{p}} 2d$$

In which V = velocity in feet per second a = area of water in square feet P = wetted perimeter in feet 2d = twice the slope in feet per mile.

Example

What is the velocity of flow in a 6-inch drain laid at a grade of ¼ inch per foot when running half full?

Solution

There is a 110-foot fall in a mile of drain laid at a grade of ¼ inch per foot.

$$V = \sqrt{\frac{.098}{.75} \times 220}$$

$$= 5.8 \text{ feet per second}$$

This water flow rate table shows water flow through pipes and copper tubing.

Volume of flow is at one foot per minute velocity in Pipe or Tube.

Schedule 40 pipe

Dia. inches	Cubic ft/min	Gallons/minute
1/8	0.0004	0.003
¼	0.0007	0.005
3/8	0.0013	0.010
½	0.0021	0.016
¾	0.0037	0.028
1	0.0062	0.046
1-¼	0.0104	0.078
1-½	0.0141	0.106
2	0.0233	0.174

The Armfield C6-MKII-10 Fluid Friction Apparatus is designed to allow the detailed study of the fluid friction head losses which occur when an incompressible fluid flows through pipes, bends, valves and pipe flow metering devices.

Friction head losses in straight pipes of different sizes can be investigated over a range of Reynolds' numbers from 10^3 to nearly 10^5, thereby covering the laminar, transitional and turbulent flow regimes in smooth pipes. A further test pipe is artificially roughened and, at the higher Reynolds' numbers, shows a clear departure from typical smooth bore pipe characteristics.

In addition to the smooth and roughened pipes, a wide range of pipeline components are fitted, including pipe fittings and control valves, allowing investigation of the losses caused by this type of connection. A clear acrylic section of pipeline houses a Venturi meter, an orifice plate assembly and a Pitot tube, so that these can be investigated as flow measurement devices.

The C6-MKII-10 is designed to be operated in conjunction with the Armfield F1-10 Hydraulics Bench. The unit can be used with a range of instrumentation packages including water and mercury manometers, hand-held digital pressure meters and a computer data logging pack.

DESCRIPTION OF EQUIPMENT

The test pipes and fittings are mounted on a tubular frame carried on castors. Water is fed in from the hydraulics bench via the barbed connector (1), flows through the network of pipes and fittings, and is fed back into the volumetric tank via the exit tube (23) (Fig. 9.2).

All numerical references relate to the diagram below.

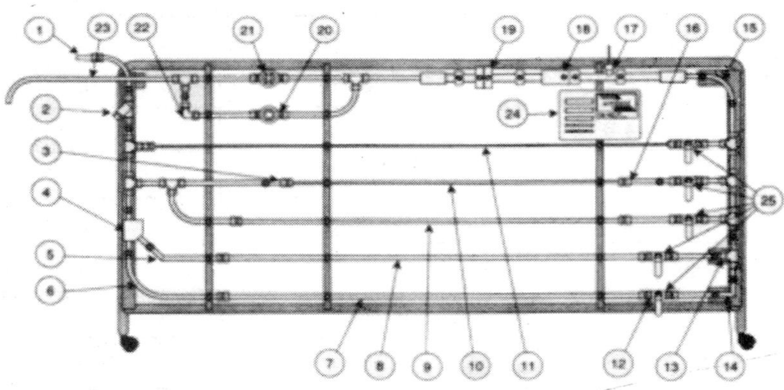

Fig. 9.2: Armfield C6-MKII-10 Fluid Friction Apparatus

The pipes are arranged to provide facilities for testing the following:

An in-line strainer (2)

An artificially roughened pipe (7)

Smooth bore pipes of 4 different diameters (8), (9), (10) and (11)

A long radius 90° bend (6)

A short radius 90° bend (15)

A 45° "Y" (4)

A 45° elbow (5)

A 90° "T" (13)

A 90° mitre (14)

A 90° elbow (22)

A sudden contraction (3)

A sudden enlargement (16)

A pipe section made of clear acrylic with a Pitot static tube (17)

A Venturi meter made of clear acrylic (18)

An orifice meter made of clear acrylic (19)

A ball valve (12)

A globe valve (20)

A gate valve (21)

Short samples of each size test pipe (24) are provided loose so that you can measure the exact diameter and determine the nature of the internal finish. The ratio of the diameter of the pipe to the distance of the pressure tappings from the ends of each pipe has been selected to minimise end and entry effects. A system of isolating valves (25) is provided whereby the pipe to be tested can be selected without disconnecting or draining the system. The arrangement also allows tests to be conducted on parallel pipe configurations. Each pressure tapping is fitted with a quick connection facility. Probe attachments with an adequate quantity of translucent polythene tubing are provided, so that any pair of pressure tappings can be rapidly connected to the pressure measurement system.

Controlling the Flow

Water is pumped through the Fluid Friction Apparatus using a centrifugal pump mounted on the inside of the hydraulics bench. The pump can be switched on and off using the switch indicated in the diagram shown in the equipment section of this web site. The Control Valve should always be closed before starting the pump.

Water flows through the connector in the channel on the bench top, through the flexible connecting hose shown in the diagram above and into the C6-MKII-10. It will then flow through whichever of the test pipes is selected, back through the acrylic pipe section and into the volumetric tank in the hydraulics bench.

Flow rates through the apparatus may be adjusted by operation of the Control Valve on the hydraulics bench. Simultaneous operation of the flow control valve with the two outlet valves (gate and globe) shown in the diagram above, will permit adjustment of the static pressure in the apparatus together with the flow rate. Using the three valves in combination, it should be possible to achieve fine adjustment of the flow if required.

Flow Path

The flow path through the pipe friction network is controlled using the system of isolating valves shown in the diagram above. By opening and closing these valves as appropriate, it is possible to select flow through any combination of pipes.

The service module incorporates a moulded volumetric measuring tank which is stepped to accommodate low or high flow rates. A stilling baffle is incorporated to reduce turbulence.

A remote sight gauge, consisting of a sight tube and scale, is connected to a tapping in the base of the tank and gives an instantaneous indication of water level. The scale is divided into two zones corresponding to the volume above and below the step in the tank.

A dump valve in the base of the volumetric tank is operated by a remote actuator. In operation, the volumetric tank is emptied by lifting the dump valve, allowing the entrained water to return to the sump. When test conditions have stabilised, the dump valve is lowered, retaining the water in the tank.

Timings are taken as the water level rises in the tank. Low flow rates are monitored on the lower portion of the scale corresponding to the small volume beneath the step. Larger flow rates are monitored on the upper scale corres-ponding to the main tank.

When very small volumetric flow rates are to be measured, the measuring cylinder supplied with the F1-10 should be used rather than the volumetric tank. When using the measuring cylinder, diversion of the flow to and from the cylinder should be synchronised as closely as possible with the starting and stopping of a watch; do not attempt to use a definite time or a definite volume.

Tapping Points

The head loss due to pipe friction is measured by taking pressure readings at different tapping points on the pipe network. In order to measure the pressure loss along a pipe, the pressure measurement device is connected between a pair of tappings, using the tubing and connectors.

Each pressure point on the apparatus is fitted with a self-sealing connection. To connect a test probe to a pressure point, simply push the tip of the test probe into the pressure point until it latches. To disconnect a test probe from a pressure point, press the metal clip of the side of the pressure point to release the test probe. Both test probe and pressure point will seal to sprevent loss of water.

Operation with Manometers

Flexible tubes are connected to the inlets at the bottom of the manometer and the quick release connectors are fitted to the other ends of the tubes. Connect the manometer tubes to the pipe network at two tappings with a high pressure drop (e.g. either side of a partially closed valve) and start the pump. Water will be forced through the manometer, expelling the air in the pipes.

When all air bubbles have been expelled, disconnect the manometer from the pipe network. The quick release fittings will seal keeping the tubes full of water. The pressurised water manometer incorporates a Schrader valve which is connected to the top manifold. This permits the levels in the limbs to be adjusted for measurement of small differential pressures at various static pressures. The hand pump will be required to effect reduction of levels at high static pressures. Alternatively the foot pump may be used.

Operation with Hand Held Pressure Meter

Fit the quick release fittings supplied with the C6-MKII-10 to the ends of the tubes on the hand held pressure meter. It is important to expel any air which may be trapped in the pipes of the pressure meter before taking readings. Connect the meter tubes to a convenient pair of tappings and switch on the pump.

Carefully undo one of the nuts holding the tubing to the pressure meter until liquid is expelled from the joint. Bleed the tube to expel any air. Tighten the nut and repeat for the other tube. When taking readings with the hand held pressure meter, it is important that the meter is zeroed before taking a set of results. Switch on the pump, close the outlet valves and then close the control valve to leave the system at a high static pressure. When the reading on the meter has stabilised, press the zero button to reset the meter.

Specifications

Test Pipe Diameters:

1. 19.1mm × 17.2mm
2. 12.7mm × 10.9mm
3. 9.5mm × 7.7mm
4. 6.4mm × 4.5mm
5. 19.1mm × 15.2mm (artificially roughened)

Distance between tappings: 1.00m

FLUID FRICTION IN A SMOOTH BORE PIPE

Objective

To determine the relationship between head loss due to fluid friction and velocity for flow of water through smooth bore pipes and to confirm the head loss friction factor.

Method

To obtain a series of readings of head loss at different flow rates ,through one or more of the smooth bore test pipes.

Theory

Professor Osborne Reynolds demonstrated that two types of flow may exist in a pipe.

1. Laminar flow at low velocities where $h \alpha u$
2. Turbulent flow at higher velocities where $h \alpha u^n$

Where h is the head loss due to friction and u is the fluid velocity, sometimes shown as v in some text books. These two types of flow are separated by a transition phase where no definite relationship between h and u exists.

Graphs of h versus u and log h versus log u show these zones.

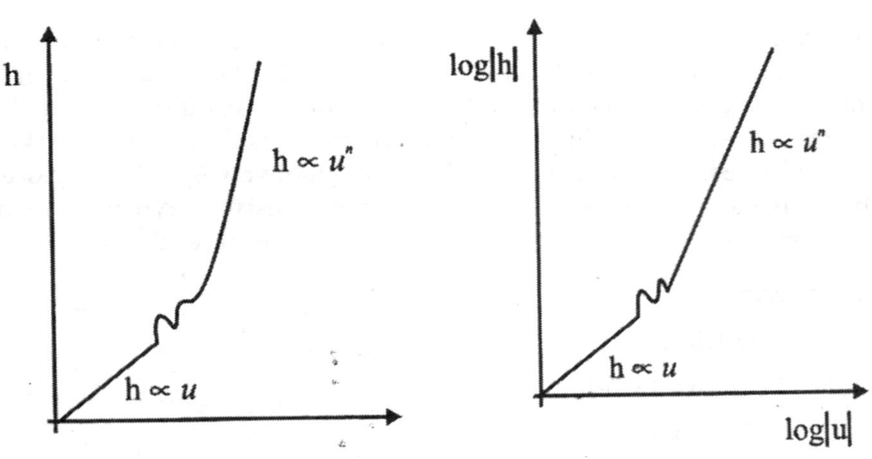

Fig. 9.3

Furthermore, for a circular pipe flowing full, the head loss due to friction may be calculated from the formula:

$$h = \frac{4fLu^2}{2gd} \quad \text{or} \quad h = \frac{\lambda Lu^2}{2gd} \qquad \text{(Eq. 9.1)}$$

(Note that some text books may show v^2 instead of u^2, but they are both the same thing.)

L is the length of the pipe between tappings,

d is the internal diameter of the pipe,

u is the mean velocity of water through the pipe in m/s,

g is the acceleration due to gravity in m/s^2 and

f is the pipe friction coefficient.

Note that the American equivalent of the British term f is λ where $\lambda = 4f$.

Reynolds' number, Re, can be found using the following equation:

$$Re = \frac{\rho ud}{\mu} \qquad \text{(Eq. 9.2)}$$

where μ is the dynamic viscosity (1.15×10^{-3} Ns/m^2 at 15°C) and r is the density (999 kg/m^3 at 15°C).

Having established the value of Reynolds' number for flow in the pipe, the value of f may be determined using a Moody diagram, a simplified version of which is shown below. You may have a more detailed version in your notes. There is also a detailed version in "Chris's web site". You will find the link in my useful links section.

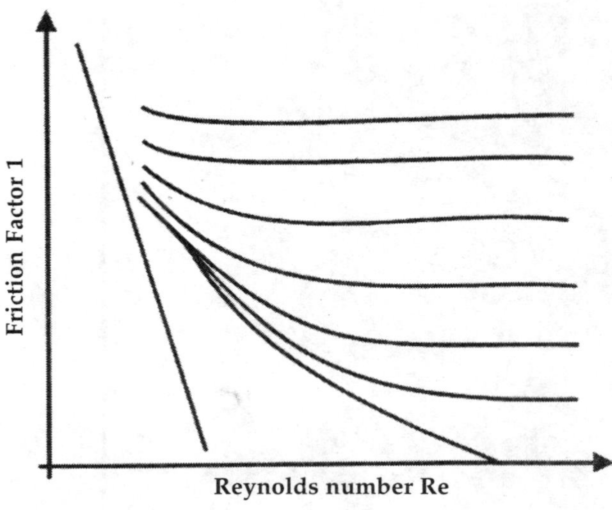

Fig. 9.4

Equation 9.1 can the be used to determine the theoretical head loss if you know the value of f for the pipe. Alternatively you can rearrange the same equation to determine f for the pipe being used in your experiment.

Equipment Set Up

Additional equipment required: Stop watch, Internal Digital Calliper.

Arrange the valves on the C6-MKII-10 to allow flow through only the test pipe under observation.

Procedure

Prime the pipe network with water. Open and close the appropriate valves to obtain flow of water through the required test pipe.

Take readings at a number of different flow rates, altering the flow using the control valve on the apparatus, (ten readings is sufficient to produce a good head-flow curve). Measure flow rates using the volumetric tank. For small flow rates use the measuring cylinder. Measure head loss between the tappings using the portable pressure meter or pressurised water manometer as appropriate.

Obtain readings on all four smooth test pipes if you have the time.

Measure the internal diameter of each test pipe sample using a Digital calliper.

10 Size of Lateral Drains

Although most drainage is applied to level land, increasingly more drainage systems are being used on sloping lands. However, sloping lands pose special problems. Unlike drainage of level lands, flow velocities and pressure can build up in drainage systems on sloping land. This can pose substantial hazards to the drainage system and to the land.

The purpose of this chapter is to direct attention to potential hazards and to measures of safeguarding against such hazards.

ASSESSMENT OF SLOPE CONDITIONS

It is imperative that all aspects of the drainage system are of the highest quality. A good plan is essential.

This permits accurate assessment of slope conditions and allows for the pinpointing of potential failure points. Plans are important, even when doing small scale installations with a backhoe.

While under-design of drain capacity on level land is of little consequence it can be disastrous on sloping land.

Severe rainstorms can temporarily overload the drains and cause the water to back up resulting in a buildup of water pressure. This rise in water pressure may force water to the surface through perforations or other openings in the line creating the potential for serious erosion.

For these reasons, main lines must never be constructed from perforated pipe. It is essential that the main lines be of adequate size, particularly at the lower end of the system, so as to comfortably accommodate heavy discharge. Connections must be fastened securely and be installed with carefully placed bedding or backfill material to hold the drain line in place.

Private Sewer

A private sewer is a drainage system serving two or more properties, which has not been adopted by the Water and Sewerage Company. A lateral drain is the section of drainage system serving a single property, which lies outside the boundary of that property.

Private sewers and lateral drains are currently the responsibility of the owners and occupiers of the properties they serve. Unless a problem occurs most householders are often unaware that they are responsible for their private sewer (sometimes jointly with others). Even where they are aware of their responsibilities, when problems do occur the costs associated with maintaining and repairing private sewers can be extremely high and are sometimes met by individuals or spread over just a few households resulting in considerable financial burdens for those responsible for them. This disparate ownership, together with a lack of planned maintenance, also means that society does not gain the benefit that integrated management of the sewerage system as a whole would bring, which is increasingly seen as important in ensuring the functionality of the system.

The UK and Welsh Assembly Government consulted on a 'Review of Existing Private Sewers and Drains in England and Wales' following which the UK and Welsh Assembly Governments concluded that transfer provided the only comprehensive solution to the problems associated with existing private sewers and lateral drains in 2003.

The UK Government and Welsh Assembly Government announced an 'in principle' decision that existing private sewers and lateral drains in England and Wales, connecting to the public sewerage network, should be transferred into the ownership of Water and Sewerage Companies on 22 Februar, 2007.

Following a joint consultation in 2007 on 'Private Sewers Transfer – Implementation Options' on possible methods for implementing the transfer of private sewer ownership, in March 2008, Defra and the Welsh Assembly Government it was clear that the majority of respondents favoured an overnight automatic transfer of ownership of private sewers and lateral drains connected to a public sewer to the statutory Water and Sewerage Companies, though response from small drainage businesses did not.

In the Summary of Response document, Defra and the Welsh Assembly Government made a commitment to draw up recommendations for implementing the transfer of private sewers and lateral drains.

UK Government announced on 15 December 2008 that from 2011 all private sewers and lateral drains that drain to the public sewerage network of water and sewerage companies in England will transfer into their ownership.

The Welsh Assembly Government's Strategic Policy Position Statement on Water, which was published on 31 March 2009, made a commitment to pursue the development of regulations in 2011 to facilitate the transfer of private sewers to water and sewerage undertakers.

A joint consultation on draft regulations and proposals for schemes for the transfer of private sewers and lateral drains to water and sewerage companies ran from August to November 2010.

The minister for environment, sustainability and housing has agreed to the publication of the government response and summary of responses to the consultation on draft regulation and proposals for schemes for the transfer of private sewers and lateral drains to water and sewerage companies in england and wales.

Water and Sewerage Undertakers can, on their initiative, or on the application of the sewer's owner, adopt existing private sewerage assets under section 102 of the Water Industry Act 1991. Section 105A of the Water Industry Act 1991, allows for Welsh Ministers, in relation to water or sewerage undertakers whose areas are wholly or mainly in Wales, to introduce schemes under which those undertakers are required to use their existing section 102 powers to adopt specified private drainage assets.

Drainage of Highway

Includes collecting, transporting, and disposing of surface/subsurface water originating on or near the highway right of way or flowing in streams crossing bordering that right of way.

Drainage of highway is important because water damage highway structure in many ways. The water which are dangerous for highways are:

- *Rainwater:* Cause erosion on surface or may seep downward and damage pavement (surface drains)
- *Groundwater:* May rise by capillary action and damage pavement (sub-surface damage)
- *Water body:* May cross a road (river/stream) and may damage road (cross drainage words)
- *Related Pages:* It is more appropriate to take care of drainage at the time of location survey.

Ideal location from a drainage stand point would lie along the divides b/w large drainage areas. Then all streams flow away from the highway, and the drainage problem is reduced to caring for the water that falls on the roadway and back slope.In contrast location paralleling large streams is far less desirable as they cross every tributary where it is largest. Ideal locations avoid steep grades and heavy cuts and fills as they create difficult.

Pavement and Shoulder

The highway engineer should ensure that the precipitation is removed from the pavement as soon as possible and that highway drainage is done efficiently. Water that falls on the road way follows laterally or obliquely from it, under the influence of cross slope. Or superelevation in pavement and shoulder.

Fig. 10.1

A suitable value of cross fall for paved roads is about 3 per cent for carriage way with a slope of 4-6 per cent for shoulders. And increased cross fall for the carriage way e.g. 4 per cent is desirable if the quantity of the final shape of the road surface is likely to be low for any reason,

Developments in Drainage Machinery and Materials

Materials for subsurface drainage systems include drainpipes and their accessories, envelope materials and auxiliary structures.

PVC and PE are generally used as pipe materials for corrugated plastic lateral drains. Concrete pipes are used for larger collector drains. Specifications and standards for clay, concrete and corrugated plastic pipes are available in the USA and in Europe a standard for corrugated PVC pipes has been drafted.

Pipe Accessories

Pipe accessories, such as end caps, couplers, pipe fittings and reducers, and rigid pipes for drain bridges and lateral outlets are also available.

Design criteria and hydraulic calculation procedures with respect to pipe diameters are well known. FAO is currently preparing simple computer programs for both single drains and multiple drains, in which the pipe diameter changes as a way to reduce material costs.

Selection of Pipe Material

The selection of pipe material and size for a particular project depends mainly on local availability and cost. In this context the following questions can be considered:

1. Are technical specifications commonly used in practice to check the quality of pipe materials used in drainage works?
2. The contribution of the pipe size to the total cost of the subsurface drainage system is relevant, however, in some cases no special attention is paid to drain diameter calculations and pipes are over-dimensioned, especially if long drains are designed.

Drain Envelopes

Drain envelopes restrict the entrance of soil particle into the drain, improve the hydraulic conductivity at the soil-drain interface and provide structural stability around the drain. Mineral granular envelopes and prewrapped fibrous organic envelopes have been used in the past, but currently synthetic envelopes -geotextiles and loose synthetic fibres- are being used.

Specifications and standards for envelope materials are also available, as well as rules and recommendations to predict the need of an envelope and design criteria for the selected material. However:

- methods validated by field experience to assess the need for drain envelopes;
- selection criteria for the most appropriate envelope material, depending on local soil conditions, need verification;

- case studies on the evaluation of the performance of drain envelopes in the field, especially for synthetic envelopes are important; and
- research activities required to support the above issues are necessary.

Auxiliary Drain Structures

Connection structures, inlets and outlets of water and special structures, such as cleaning facilities and structures for controlled drainage and subirrigation, are common auxiliary structures of subsurface drainage systems.

In the academic discussion, the following issues can be covered:

- Quality control and maintenance of outlet structures.
- In composite drainage systems, junction boxes and manholes are sometimes hardly used or not used at all and may be unnecessary with GPS availability. Examples with practical data about the comparison of savings in construction costs and increments in maintenance costs may be useful for future designs.
- Designs for special structures for controlled drainage in the lateral and collector outlets are available, but examples of construction and operation of such structures are not frequent.

Use of Trenchers

Trenchers of various types have been used in the past and still are used with success to install subsurface drains, especially for clay and concrete pipes and for granular mineral envelopes. Since the introduction of corrugated plastic pipes and prewrapped envelope materials, the installation speed has increased by using trenchless drainage machines.

However, although the use of the laser grade has improved the precision of installation, the control of the work quality has become more difficult, especially as far as the grade line accuracy is concerned.

Suggested topics for papers describing new developments and for discussion may be the following:

- Installation of drains under adverse conditions, such as in wet soils and in lands with shallow water tables.
- Subsurface drainage works in unstable soils.
- Checking the quality of drainage work during installation and after the drainage system has been installed.

Drainage Materials

Subsurface drainage systems adequately installed with appropriate drainage materials have low maintenance requirements. Dry rodding is sufficient to remove slight clogging, fresh ochre and roots proliferating inside the drainpipe, specially near the lateral outlet. To remove sediments and serious ochre deposits, and to clean clogged perforations jet flushing is necessary. Field experience achieved during the past years shows that medium pressure equipment is most recommended and flushing should be used only in case of dissatisfaction with or deterioration of drainage system performance.

The effective length of the flushing equipment is less than about 400 m. Therefore, this technology is effective for single drains with lengths up to 400 m and for multiple drains if manholes are constructed. However, extended laterals and composite drainage systems are sometimes installed without manholes. In these cases, are there other effective cleaning facilities or procedures?

TREES AND CROP PRODUCTION

Trees can grow on agricultural land in many useful and profitable ways. These include: windbreaks, treed fence rows, fruit and nut orchards, stream buffers, shelter for pastures, shelter for farm buildings, plantations, woodlots and reforested marginal land. Cropped farm fields and pastures are often under-drained with tile to remove excess water to enhance crop production. Some species of trees can aggressively plug farm drain tiles with roots while other tree species rarely plug drains. If conditions are favourable, it is believed that any tree species has the ability to plug farm drains with roots. Where crop production is to continue, tree planting projects on drained land must be designed to sustain the use of tile drains and not interfere with removal of excess field water.

Properly Designed Drainage System

A properly designed drainage system should quickly remove water from farm soil whenever an excess amount of water is present. Excess soil water can occur any time of year, however, is typically most abundant from late winter to early spring, late summer to early winter and sporadically during the growing season due to heavy or prolonged rains. The need for field drainage can vary from season to season. Field tiles that have remained fairly dry for several years may run water frequently or constantly during wet seasons if water tables become high. Tiles that drain natural springs will always run water. During most seasons, farmers realize production advantages by having field drains in place.

Drain lines blocked by tree roots will disrupt proper water drainage. How can this problem affect crop production? Winter melt water and spring rains may not drain adequately to allow early tilling and seeding especially on heavy soils. Wet soils are cooler and can delay crop germination and growth, reducing crop yields. Sporadic summer flooding can remain pooled too long in low spots, resulting in crop damage. In late summer and fall, soil may be too soft to permit heavy harvest equipment onto the land. It costs time and money to locate the plug and replace it with new pipe. Farmers depend on a functional drainage system to remove excess field water.

Farm Drainage

Farm drainage is a production investment that can cost $600/acre to install. Tree plantings added to farmland can also be designed as production investments. In order to establish trees and shrubs on farmland in beneficial ways without risk of plugging drain tiles with roots, recommendations on tile drain installation are outlined in OMAFRA Publication 29, Drainage Guide for Ontario. These recommendations have been established through field experience and are recognized by drainage contractors. If questions on tile and tree root plugging arise, farmers should consult with their drainage contractor or OMAFRA Agricultural Engineer.

Precautions for Stream (Riparian) Buffers

Where trees, shrubs and weeds associated with wet soils are established or are permitted to grow naturally along a watercourse, perforated tile that passes under the buffer to an outlet can quickly become plugged by roots. For field tiles that drain into buffered streams, intermittent watercourses or ditches, a section of non-perforated tile should be installed.

The non-perforated section of tile should extend from the outlet, pass under the vegetated buffer, and continue for at least 15 metres into the cultivated field where it can then connect to standard perforated pipe. Roots will not penetrate non-perforated pipe. Worry-free drainage of field water will continue with added benefits realized by having buffered vegetated watercourses.

How Tree Roots Grow in the Soil

Roots of trees grow to new areas of soil to increase the root surface area. Nutrient uptake, water absorption and anchorage are key functions of roots. Roots grow proportionately in size with the above ground tree and maintain a specific root-to-shoot ratio. Roots of many species of trees, some weeds, several shrub and crop species can grow close to and within tile drains as they expand their ability to acquire water and nutrients.

Back-filled soil over drainage tiles provides easy access for roots to the tile due to the breakup of compacted soil layers and loosening of the back-filled soil by the drainage installation equipment. Roots do not actively search the soil for moisture and nutrients but grow more vigorously as they randomly encounter more favorable growing conditions such as, increased moisture and nutrient levels. Root growth conditions can continue to improve until moisture becomes excessive or nutrients reach toxic levels at which point root growth declines.

The ideal amount of soil moisture or the ideal amount of each nutrient is entirely dependent upon the tree species. Physical soil properties can become more favorable for root growth with increasing moisture. Roots may develop more vigorously towards an increasing humidity gradient and moisture gradient. Roots can push their way through soil easier towards an increasing moisture gradient as soil becomes more pliable due to increasing amounts of water. Other soil factors such as oxygen concentrations and soil particle size also contribute to ease of root growth.

How Tree Roots Plug Drain Tiles

Drainage tiles that are perforated with holes (modern plastic pipe), have gaps (sectional clay tile) or are damaged by cracks can be plugged by roots. Non-perforated pipe cannot be plugged by roots since there are no entry points. Roots are more likely to be found within tile after a prolonged dry period as root systems expand downward to increase their ability to absorb water.

A root will likely stop growing once it enters a dry tile but can remain alive. The root will not proliferate to plug the tile if the root does not encounter a water source. Once running water or standing water becomes available inside a tile, tree roots that are present may proliferate and plug the tile. The rate of root growth and an ability to plug is dependent on the species of the root occupying the tile. Roots will plug tile slower if other sources of water are available outside the tile during the same period of time.

Problems of Drainage

Drainage problems are first noticed by the farmer as a wet spot in a field that does not drain as fast as it did in previous seasons or as an area of unhealthy crop. Upon inspection of tile outlets water may be observed running later in the spring and early summer. The late water flow may not be due to 'late flowing water' but can be due to a slow leak in the plug itself. A backup of water up the tile system may simply be taking a much longer time to drain.

The root growth which created the plug could have progressed the previous season in early autumn and continued as late as December. The plug may have developed over several seasons. An old tile system may be losing the ability to effectively drain the land due to accumulations of sediment or pipe collapse. Plugged sections of tile will need to be located, cut out and a new section of tile spliced into the line.

Root masses that form within tile can occasionally break free from the parent plant and travel downstream inside the tile, eventually blocking water flow at a different location. These shifting plugs have been found blocking drains of interconnected neighbouring farms causing crop damage. Determining where the root mass originated from can sometimes be difficult.

Water can run through tile constantly or it can flow for an extended duration into the growing season due to drainage of natural springs or drainage of areas in a field where the water table meets a tile. Indication of this water flow can usually be observed at the tile outlet.

Depth to the water table can vary from one season to the next and is dependent upon seasonal rainfall patterns. Tiles that are dry during average growing seasons may have late flow of water during wet seasons. Field locations having wet tile will be a risky area to establish any tree species since plugging by roots may eventually occur.

Water may be running through sections of field drainage later into the growing season but may not be realized by the farmer. Tile can drain water from an up-slope, wet area or from a spring however, as the water makes its way down the tile to drier areas the water can leave the tile through perforations. The water can re-enter the soil in another area before reaching the drain outlet. In these situations, and unknown to a farmer, trees planted close to tiles that have standing or flowing water could cause root-plugging problems.

At a low field elevation, plugging in tile by roots may encourage proliferation of roots of other trees upstream in the line since water remains present until the plug is noticed and subsequently released.

How Trees Remove Soil from Soil?

By transpiration, trees, like crops, can remove significant amounts of water from soil. If planted dense enough, could trees act as an effective natural substitute for tile drainage on farmland? Trees remove little soil water during times of critical farming activities. In order to remove soil water through transpiration, water must evaporate through photosynthesizing deciduous leaves or needles of conifers. Trees remove water from soil when crops absorb water from soil, during the growing season, from mid-spring to early autumn. At other times of the year, trees transpire very little water out of the soil. Although some moisture evaporates from trees during winter dormancy, the amount is small. Trees remove very little water from soil before early spring and after mid-autumn since leaves are absent or are no longer functional, and for most conifers, needles are either ending or beginning their winter dormant period. Early spring and fall are critical times when land needs to be drained to allow access by heavy farm equipment. Field tile will adequately drain field water at these important times.

During heavy summer rains and occasional flooding, soil oxygen levels can be depleted enough to cause many tree species to stop water uptake altogether, especially dry-site trees. Tree species that tolerate wet soil and are able to continue absorbing water during floods would not remove field water fast enough to enable nearby crops to survive the prolonged saturated conditions. Trees will not function as a natural substitute for tile drainage during sporadic saturation of farm soil during the growing season.

11 Open Drains

Many farmers have constructed deep, open drains on their properties. These drains are generally excavated by a back hoe or a bulldozer. Whilst the farmers are prepared to pay for and construct these drains, land-holders further downstream are usually unhappy about receiving the extra saline water that flows in the drains. They are also concerned about sediments carried in the water. The result of this conflict has been bitterness between some land-holders. To reduce these conflicts and the degradation of land downstream, drainage regulations were introduced in 1992.

During rain or irrigation, the agricultural fields become wet. The water infiltrates into the soil and is stored in its pores. When all the pores are filled with water, the soil is said to be saturated and no more water can be absorbed; when rain or irrigation continues, pools may form on the soil surface.

Some part of the water present in the saturated upper soil layers flows downward into deeper layers and is replaced by water infiltrating from the surface pools.

When there is no more water left on the soil surface, the downward flow continues for a while and air re-enters in the pores of the soil. This soil is not saturated anymore.

Our home is perhaps one of our most precious possessions. But is it enough to boast of a beautifully decorated interior? Think again! The external look of our dwelling place appeals visually but what's going on underneath the foundation is often much more important. The drainage system of any abode needs equal attention in order to provide sustainability and safety.

DRAINAGE SYSTEM

Drainage is the natural or artificial removal of surface and sub-surface water from an area. A smart drainage solution is mandatory to dissipate surplus water both in farming lands and in residential areas. Untreated excess water abets the chances of erosion of the foundation, making the structure of your home unstable. On the other hand agricultural soil needs drainage to enhance production or to manage water supplies.

An underground drainage system comprises of pipes and storage tanks made from perforated wall modules to form the desired size and configuration. They are wrapped in a water permeable geotextile. The system is preferably buried in clean sand, whereby rainwater and runoff water is directed to flow through the water permeable geotextile.

Drainage can be either natural or artificial. Many areas have some natural drainage which means that excess water flows from the farmers' fields to swamps or to lakes and rivers. Natural drainage, however, is often inadequate and artificial or man-made drainage is required.

Surface drainage is the process of removal of excess water from the surface of the land. This is normally accomplished by shallow ditches which are also called open drains. The shallow ditches discharge into larger and deeper collector drains. In order to facilitate the flow of excess water towards the drains, the field is given an artificial slope by means of land grading.

Subsurface drainage is the removal of water from the root zone. It is accomplished by deep open drains or buried pipe drains. Excess water from the root zone flows into the deep open drains. The disadvantage of this type of subsurface drainage is that it makes the use of machinery difficult. Pipe drains are buried pipes with openings through which the soil water can enter. The pipes convey the water to a collector drain.

Drainage system that lies beneath your home works hard at all time to keep your abode prim and proper. Not only does it have to process water waste that is created by bathing and washing dishes, but it also handles sewage waste and outside water that is draining off your home. This is a tough set of responsibilities for the residential underground drainage system to handle so you might want to think proactively about keeping this system in working order.

Under these regulations "farmers must notify the Commissioner of Soil and Land Conservation of their intention to drain or pump water for the control of salinity" so that anyone likely to be affected is informed.

In April 1995, Agriculture WA undertook a stock-quality drilling programme in the North Stirling area. Three of the selected sites were on

Mr. Ken Pech's farms which form the headwaters of the Six Mile Creek. Ken showed us the deep drains he had constructed more than ten years earlier. His photos showed that there was an apparent reduction in salinity in an area between 100 and 200 m away from the drains. The improvements were unusual because similarly constructed drains in other landforms have had little or no effect on the salinity status of their surrounding areas. We decided to evaluate these drains and present the results for the benefit of other land-holders that may want to construct deep drains.

Methods

Geological description of the area were based on:

(*a*) soil profile information from three bores which were drilled. the drilling logs for two of these bores, which are typical of the profiles in the area.

(*b*) the rocks found in the area were Pallinup Siltstone and spongolite, both of which are of Tertiary origin, and a few Precambrian basement rocks (found in the upper section of the drain).

(*c*) descriptions of soil profiles along the drain

We recorded the position of major seepage zones which were along the mid section of the drain.

Aerial photographs from 1985 and 1993 were interpreted to find the extent of saltaffected land before, and eight years after, construction of the drains.

The length of the drain was measured from the 1993 aerial photographs. We contacted a local contractor to obtain current construction costs. These quotes are related to the size of drains.

In December 1996, we walked along the drains and:

- Noted which areas were strongly salt-affected (had become bare grounds);
- Used a Geonic EM38 instrument to define the salinity status of the suspected areas (using the relation given in Ferdowsian and Greenham, 1992);
- Described four typical soil profiles ,
- Estimated the flow rate at several sites ;
- Sampled the baseflow to measure its salinity.

Results

Geology and Soil Material

The area is covered by Pallinup Siltstone which is a Tertiary Formation. The Pallinup sediments in this area, are mainly composed of fine silt, clay and occasionally fine to medium sand. The siltstone, in some areas, contains pink and white spongolite (a siltstone full of sponge spicules).

The Pallinup Siltstone overlays the basement rock which is of Precambrian origin and part of the Yilgarn Craton. There are basement (granite and gneiss) highs in the area that are covered by sediments. Weathered granite can be seen along the bed of the main drain.

Drain Specification

The drainage system is composed of one main drain (6.5 km) and 7 km of lateral ones. The main drain and a few of the laterals (8 km altogether) were constructed in 1984. Another 4.5 km of lateral drains were constructed in 1985 and 1986. Only one lateral drain (about 1 km) was constructed after 1993 and so this cannot be seen on the 1993 aerial photographs.

All drains have a trapezoidal cross-section. The bed of the main drain is 3 m wide and its sideslopes 1:1 (vertical : horizontal). The beds of lateral drains are 1.2 m wide and their sideslopes 2:1. With the exception of approximately 100 m; the granite high near M6), the drains are entirely in the Pallinup Formation.

Condition of the Drain

With the exception of a few places, the sideslopes of the lateral drains are stable have not collapsed. The large piles of spoils are bare and exposed to erosion.

Coarse grains of sand could be seen along the banks of the lateral drains which indicate that the spoils from the lateral drains have been eroded and entered the drains.

Some sections of the main drain were badly eroded. Gullies, 1 m apart and up to 0.5 m deep, had formed along the sideslopes in some sections of the main drain. Part of the eroded material had filled the base of the main drain and part was transported out of the area. There were also indications of sedimentation further downstream. A typical site where this silting may be seen is 500 m before the creek crosses the South Formby Road. On the 1985, aerial photographs there are four pools in this area. These pools are absent on the 1993 aerial photographs. It is likely that these pools have been filled with silt between 1985 and 1993. Silting of the creek bed can also be seen further downstream, east of the South Formby Road.

Flow rates, baseflow salinity, evaporation along the drainage system and salt export. The bed of the drain was wet throughout its entire length but only a few seepage areas which had sandy profiles contributed to the baseflow. Seepage zones included sections of the drain which had been cut into the floor of salt lakes.

The flow rate along the main drain (December 1996) varied between 0.2 L/sec and 2 L/sec (M1; at the outlet of the property). A few of the lateral drains had no or little flow. The flowing water was baseflow which was ground water seeping into the drain.

Baseflow salinity varied between 5600 and 8400 mS/m. The lowest salinity reading (5600 mS/m) was at site L5 which is close to a seepage zone.

This salinity is probably similar to the salinity of the groundwater. The salinity of the baseflow at the outlet of the property was 8300 mS/m. The increase in salinity is probably due to evaporation.

The ratio of baseflow salinity at the outlet of the property (8300 mS/m) and the lowest salinity (5600 mS/m) shows salt concentration due to evaporation along the drainage system. Thus without evaporation, the flow rate at the outlet of the property (Q) would be:

$$Q = 2\ \text{L/sec} \times 8300/5600 \text{ or } Q = 3\ \text{L/sec}$$

The base flow was carrying approximately 7.9 tonnes of salt out of the property each day in December 1996. We expect that the salt export will probably be much higher during winter months. Silberstein (1989) found that the average salt export, at the outlet of the drainage system, was approximately 240 tonnes per day, between 10 th May and 30th July 1988. The annual salt export figure was 120 tonnes per day during 1988. He attributed the large salt export to the excessive runoff which was the result of an exceptionally wet season. The total rain falling during May, June, and July 1988 was 287 mm, compared to the 10 year average of 144 mm for the same period.

Lewis (1992) studied the North Stirling Basin, which is west of the study area. Average salt storages in the 13 bores which she studied were 1830 t/ha (average depth 13.50 m). Salt stored in the drain's catchment (9600 ha) would probably be the same as reported by Lewis.

Assuming that the drain would continue to remove 7.9 tonnes of salt each day, it will take more than 6000 years for the drain to remove all of the salt from the soil profile. Even with the highest salt export rates (120 tonnes per day; in 1988), it would take about 200 years to flush half of the stored salt from the catchment of the study area.

Water Balance and Potential Salinity

We expect that between 10 mm (in a year with average rainfall) and 50 mm (in a decile 8 year; two wettest years out of ten) of the annual rainfall would recharge the aquifer each year. If we assume that the catchment boundaries are the same as the aquifer boundaries, then the total area that contributes to the base flow in the drain will be 9600ha. The annual base flow out of the property and evaporation along the drainage system is 94,600 m 3 (3 L/sec) which is less than 1 mm per year over the total catchment area. The rate of base flow discharge is very little compared with the recharge under pastures and crops. Thus, the deep drain alone will not stop soil salinity and many more areas may eventually become salt-affected. As an example, area 1, has become saline since 1993.

Effect of the Deep Drain on the Extent of the Salt-Affected Area

In this report, salt-affected areas are defined as lands that have become bare and appear as highly reflective areas on the aerial photographs. These areas do not include moderately or slightly salt-affected areas (barley grass areas or salt-affected cropping land).

About 251 ha of land was strongly salt-affected on the 1985 aerial photographs. These areas looked continuous and spread out. Most of the affected areas were in the natural drainage beds.

The total salt-affected area based on 1993 aerial photographs was about 224 ha. By comparing the 1985 and 1993 aerial photographs, we could see that:

- salt-affected areas close to the deep drains had been reduced, and in some places had become isolated; and
- during the same period, salinity had encroached into other areas that were further away from the drain.

We found that the salt-affected land in the study area had reduced by 27 ha between 1985 and 1993. Out of the 27 ha which showed signs of improvement, about 8 ha was cropped in 1996 and the balance (19 ha) was within the natural creek beds and flood plains.

Improvement of creek beds and flood plains could be partly attributed to them being fenced off and revegetated with salt-tolerant species. These areas had been mounded and planted with salt-tolerant species. Melaleuca thyoides, Acacia saligna and Atriplex spp. were among the surviving plants. Melaleuca thyoides was very impressive with a large canopy (5 m in diameters) and healthy growth.

The improved area, furthest from the drain which was cropped in 1996 was a 3 ha patch of land) up to 200 m away from the main drain. Improvement of this land is entirely due to the effects of the drain since there is no treatment other than the drain. The area was bare in 1985. This area had been cropped but not harvested because the crop (barley) looked patchy.

The Geonic EM38 readings on this area were between 80 and 120mS/m. These reading showed that the area was still moderately salt affected. This land is probably on a sandy lens that crosses the deep drain. By having a high hydraulic conductivity, this sandy lens has extended the effect of the drain far beyond the expected distance. We observed one section of the deep drain that had higher seepage rates than other areas and found that the sandy lens crossed the drain here.

Feasibility of the Deep Drain

The Net Present Value (NPV) is a measure used in economic analysis to determine a project's net benefits. It is the discounted value of expected benefits, less the discounted value of expected costs. The Net Present Value of the drain has been calculated based on the following assumptions:

- Drain construction cost $30,000 (1985);
- No maintenance until year 2000;
- Benefits from construction of drains commence in 1989;
- Barley grown on reclaimed area;
- Barley gross margin $130/ha.

The analysis indicated that at a discount rate of 8 per cent the investment cost would be recovered if 40 ha of land was reclaimed. The actual reclaimed area (8 ha) will not recover costs over the life of the project. The area required to break even varies with the level of discount rate.

The analysis does not account for off-site effects of the drain such as export of salt and silt to the other properties. It also does not account for intangible gains or losses such as the scenic values of reclaiming land, look of the drain with its spoil mounds and access to paddocks.

Unhygienic and Unsafe Open Drains

A huge open drain. manholes that seem to be sinking, which keep overflowing at intervals. Roads that get flooded with sewage when it rains. A perennial stink. This can best describe Palmgrove Road.

It's the broad road off the busy Victoria Road in the Central Business District, where the real estate rates are steadily climbing. And yet Palm

Grove Road has been neglected by the civic authorities. The old area had its sewage lines laid over 100 years ago.

The ancient, leaky pipes are not just corroded but clogged with garbage and sewage does not flow freely through the lines. The road is dotted with manholes, which overflow every now and then. Many manholes on the perpendicular Victoria Road have begun to sink. It gets worse when it rains. The drainage system fills beyond its capacity and sewage mixed with rainwater floods the road and many apartment complexes that line this road.

Residents of the road have covered many manholes with large stone slabs to keep the lids in place. This, however, does not stop the sewage from flowing out on to the road. There is a huge open drain along the road. It crosses the breath of the road in the middle and flows along the other side of the road.

The drain is left open. The water level in the open drain is high and heavy rain and an assortment of garbage is enough to fill it up. Residents living in the apartments facing the drain requested the BBMP several times to close the drain. They were told that the drain could not be closed, as de-silting work was planned. "We did not see any de-silting happening, but the drain remained open. It is unhygienic and unsafe. Though there is a wall and a fence along most parts of the drain, the wall is not high and children might fall into it. Moreover, it is an ugly sight.

However, saturation may have lasted too long for the plants' health. Plant roots require air as well as water and most plants cannot withstand saturated soil for long periods However, rice is an exception.

Besides damage to the crop, a very wet soil makes the use of machinery difficult, if not impossible.

The water flowing from the saturated soil downward to deeper layers, feeds the groundwater reservoir. As a result, the groundwater level.

12 Drainage of Barnyards and Cattle-Lanes

The stockman is familiar with the difficulties to be met in keeping ground which becomes puddled by the frequent tramping of live stock from becoming exces sively muddy. Such ground cannot be materially benefited by placing tile drains underneath the puddled surface. The remedy consists in preventing all water from outside sources from finding its way to the yard, leaving only the direct rainfall to be contended with.

The roof water from all buildings adjoining the yards should be taken care of by eaves-troughs, and downspouts which should conduct the water either into cisterns or into a tile drain provided for the purpose.

This receiving drain should be laid around the buildings and discharge into some open channel or into a system of field drains. A tile of 8-inch diameter will carry the roof water from a large barn, and may discharge into a field main without overcharging it, for the reason that in all heavy rainfalls the roof water will have passed through the drain before soil water will have had time to enter. It is not desirable that stock-yards should be kept dry by surface drainage unless the value of the manure is to be disregarded. It is the practice of many good farmers to so arrange the stock-yards that all rainfall will gravitate toward the center, which thereby becomes the receptacle for valuable manures and gives drainage to the outer parts of the yard. In all cases the surface water from surrounding land should be cut off by shallow trenches supplemented by under drains.

These suggestions, if followed, will result in a great amelioration of the mud evil so often endured by farmers and stockmen under the impression that there is no remedy for the knee-deep conditions of their yards.

No surface water should be permitted to enter tile drains direct unless precautions are taken to prevent mud and debris from entering the drain. It is frequently desirable to remove surface water by means of underdrains from certain places which are not susceptible to drainage by soil filtration nor provided with surface-drain outlets. Some of these are ponds or depressions by the roadside, yards which are kept closely compacted by constant use, drainage from carriage washes and barns which is charged with muddy material, and other like necessities.

For such purposes, the catch-basin will serve an excellent purpose. It is a well constructed with brick, 3 feet in diameter, with a depth of 2 feet below the outlet pipe for the settling of mud and heavy material which should be removed whenever the space below the discharge is filled. The discharge pipe should not be less than 6 inches in diameter in any case and should not be connected with any extensive field system, but should extend direct to some large outlet. The inlet should be 10 or 12 inches in diameter and have two rods placed vertically through drilled holes near the entrance to serve as a screen. Both inlet and outlet pipes should be vitrified sewer-pipes to withstand the effects of freezing, which common clay ware will not. A wooden box instead of a brick well will serve the same purpose, but must be renewed when the wood decays, and is obviously less permanent as an improvement. In some respects, however, the wood construction is more desirable.

The inlet may then be a hole in the side of the box at the surface flow line, with iron rods fastened vertically across it.

A serviceable and easily constructed catch-basin may be made of the sections of 24-inch sewer-pipe, which should be set end to end in a vertical position and the socket joints secured by cement mortar. The bottom section should be a straight pipe, the upper two sections should have T's, one of which should be used for an outlet and the other for an inlet. A 2-inch plank cover fitted and dropped into the top socket finnishes a neat and desirable catch-basin.

Catch-basin constructed of Sewer-pipe. These catch-basins will require some personal attention at times. Straws and other surface rubbish from the surface ditch will gather against the inlet and must be removed. The mud which accumulates in the bottom of the basin should be removed from time to time. It is, however, a useful and convenient accessory to drainage work.

PROCEDURE TO CONSTRUCT TILE DRAIN

Cellars which are excavated in clay or loam soils usually become wet and require drainage. A common method of procedure is to construct a tile drain to carry the water away after it enters the cellar. Another is to cover the walls and bottom with a thick coat of cement mortar to prevent water from entering. If ihere is much soil water to contend with, it frequently bursts through the coating used in the latter method, and when the former is used, the cellar remains damp even when the drain removes the free water which percolates through the soil and finds its way to the low point in the bottom from which drainage is made.

The proper plan to follow is to prevent water from entering by means of a tile drain, which should be laid entirely around the building 4 or 5 feet distant from the walls and nearly if not quite as deep as the floor of the cellar. This drain should be of 4-inch tile laid on an even fall of one inch in 16 feet, and connect with a main which will carry the drainage safely aay from the house. By this method the ground about the house as well as the cellar will be kept dry and wholesome, and is the best known plan for securing a dry cellar for a country house where natural drainage is deficient.

The underdrainage of the ground occupied by buildings and surrounding yards and gardens is often neglected on the supposition that these grounds have sufficient natural drainage, which is not always the case.

Filtration and Water Supply

The filtration of all surface water through the soil of the lawn, garden, and surrounding grounds in general, and its removal by the process of underdrainage, will add much to the ease with which walks may be constructed and maintained, and to the satisfactory growth of all useful and ornamental plants which contribute so largely to the beauty, value and healthfulness of a country residence.

The water supply is usually taken from a well located near the residence. While the supply of this well may have its source in a vein of clay, and be all that is desired in point of purity and coolness, it is subject to contamination by surface and soil water which percolates through the earth and finds lodgment in the well. Some deep under drains laid about the well will prevent the pollution of the water from this source where the wells are located on level or undulating tracts of land.

Barnyard Drainage

Nothing can be more discouraging to both beginning and experienced graziers than having to cope with muddy cows. But the good news is there are many cost-effective ways to keep cows clean, even during soggy spring weather.

While mud is a particular concern for dairy farmers, beef and sheep producers also need to pay attention to proper laneway planning and management says Rob DeClue, conservationist with the Chenango County

SWCD and Graze-NY technical specialist. "You can have great forage ready to graze. But if you can't get the animals to the paddocks, it won't do you any good," observes DeClue. "For many graziers, laneways are the weak link in their grazing system, and when the going gets muddy some of them give up."

Many of the potential benefits of grazing—such as less prep time before milking and fewer foot - and udder problems—won't be realized if your cows have to waste energy slogging through the mud getting to and from the barn, he adds. "Plus the general public—which is concerned about animal welfare—associates clean animals with happy animals," he observes.

DeClue offers these farmer-tested tips:

- *Start at the barn door:* What good are great laneways if your barnyard is a mess? Be sure to channel roof water and divert other runoff away from loafing areas.
- *Invest up close first:* Focus your efforts on high-traffic laneways close to the barnyard. Management—not money —might be a better way to tackle wet spots farther out in your grazing system. For example, plan to mechanically harvest paddocks that may be tough to reach in spring without forcing your stock through muddy spots.
- *Plan ahead:* When setting up your grazing system, skirt wet spots when you locate your laneways. Recall places where existing pastures were slow to drain or cropland was often too wet to work, and route laneways around them. Where your stock must cross draws, intermittent streams or hollows that are wet after storms, consider building a stabilized, durable crossing.
- *Turn the problem into the solution:* Where hardpan soils limit drainage, you can often remove the topsoil, bulldoze the subsoil to form a raised lane, then grade and crown it so that surface water flows away from the path.
- *Beef-up high traffic areas:* Lanes close to the barn take a constant beating. They may require more intensive work, says DeClue. He recommends this strategy: First, excavate the top foot or so of soil from the lane. Then line the area with geotextile fabric, fill with coarse aggregate (such as clean bank-run gravel or equivalent), crown above the original grade, top with 1-inch or so of mixed-size crusher dust or lime dust, then roll. The dust acts as a weak cement to help bind the larger aggregates. The cohesive surface helps prevent cows from tracking stones onto concrete pads where they can cause stone bruises.

In a recent posting on the graze-l internet discussion group, Ohio dairyman F.W. Owen described how he avoids stone bruises by substituting the tabs punched out from asphalt shingles, available free for the hauling from a local factory. Other farmers suggested cushiony "chips" made from old tires that are often available locally. But they also cautioned to avoid those that may be contaminated with metal fibers from steel-belted tires and to check with local environmental authorities first.

Many farmers are tempted to skip the geotextile fabric, which keeps the animals from punching the aggregate down into the soil. But in DeClue's experience, the relatively low cost of the material (usually about \$.60 to \$.90 per running foot for 12.5-foot wide stock, depending on the type used) is worth it, in most cases. "Barring native gravel, a tough hard pan or bedrock near the surface, it's just a matter of time before the aggregate will get swallowed up, and you'll have to haul in more," he explains. As the muck oozes up from below, animals also are more prone to bruise their feet on the embedded stones.

- *Rotate laneways:* Many farmers have minimized mud problems by building double-wide laneways close to the barn, splitting them down the middle, and alternating from side to side as needed. Sometimes it might be necessary to form a temporary lane with portable fence along the inside edge of a paddock or major subdivision to route cows around a wet spot in the permanent laneway.

  In the far reaches of your grazing system, DeClue suggests building a single permanent "backbone" fence instead of two laneway fences. Form a lane with temporary fence on one side of the backbone to reach paddocks on that side, then flip the lane to the other side to reach the other paddocks. On remote laneways that don't get much use, the sod may be tough enough to support cows even when it's wet, assuming that they'll only need to use the lane a few times before extended rest.

- *Watch your water:* Locating water tanks in your laneway increases traffic in the lane and can lead to more mud problems. Water distribution systems that feed movable tanks connected to strategically placed hydrants with 50 to 75 feet of above-ground hose allow you rotate and rest areas muddied up by the animals.

- *Watch your weight:* Keep tractors and heavy equipment off of your livestock lanes — especially when it's wet — or build a heavier-duty lane designed to take more punishment.

- *Seek help:* Technical assistance and cost-sharing is available for many of these strategies.

"Sometimes the money you spend making improvements doesn't look good going out," says Lee Wilson, dairyman and NYPA chair. "But the cows sure look better coming in."

Kill two birds with one stone Peter Mapstone, who grazes 100 cows and heifers in Manlius, N.Y., found a creative solution to mud problems that keeps his cows' feet dry and their thirst quenched. Mapstone had a neighbour skim the clay off a perennially wet spot at the top of a hill, excavate the underlying shale to form a nearly half-acre pond, and relined it with the clay. After the 12-foot-deep pond filled, Mapstone used 1.5-inch plastic pipe to gravity feed the water to his pastures and barn. The neighbor also formed a half-mile 1- to 2-foot thick lane by grading and rolling the excavated shale. "The shale is sharp but it's pretty soft. There's a lot of dirt mixed in with it so it's a lot like crusher-run. The roller packed it down hard with no sharp edges sticking up," says Mapstone. "It works great. The cows never sink in more than an inch." Mapstone also used some of the shale in his barnyard, and sold some to help pay for the project.

Managing Outdoor Confinement Areas and Livestock Yards

An outdoor confinement area (OCA) is defined by the regulation as an enclosure for livestock or game animals that has all of the following characteristics:

- an unroofed area, with the exception of small wind or shade shelters that are under 20 m^2(200 ft^2). Such shelters are considered part of the OCA
- permanent or portable feeding or watering equipment
- a grazing or foraging area that accounts for less than 50 per cent of the animal's dry matter intake
- fences, pens, corrals or similar structures to confine the animals that are either permanent or temporary
- access to a barn. The non-roofed area may be an OCA.

Some livestock yards or paddocks might not meet all of the characteristics of an OCA. For example, grazing systems, including crop residues, and true pastures are not OCAs.

Permanent OCAs

A permanent OCA (POCA) is a site with the characteristics listed above where the animals:

- have access to it for at least 200 days/year or 2,400 hours in a 365 day period; or
- are present less than 200 days, but there are 300 or more nutrient units (NUs) annually in the area and stocking density is greater than five NUs per hectare on an annualized basis (5 NU/hectare/yr.) in the confinement area.

The Regulation defines nutrient units and lists (in Table 12.1) various species, animal sizes and the number of each it takes to generate one NU. See the nutrient management section of the ministry website for more information as well as the complete nutrient management tables for the Regulation. Below is an example of nutrient unit calculations.

Table 12.1: Sample Calculations of Nurtrient Units

Livestock	Nutrient unit conversion factor in the NM Tables)	Nutrient Units
100 beef backgrounders	3	33
10 medium frame horses	1	10
Total Nutrient Units	43	

A benefit to fitting under the definition of a POCA is that the rules related to siting, management of manure and snow containing manure are governed by Part VII of the Regulation.

The sheep have access to the adjacent barn whereas the cattle will rest on the mounded manure and straw mound in the background. While there are other notable differences, such as a concrete floor for the sheep compared to the cattle that have a dirt floor, both pictures represent permanent OCAs.

An open-air lamb feedlot with a barn and a yard equipped with a fence-line. The yard is an example of a permanent OCA

Livestock Yards that are Not Permanent OCAs

There are many livestock yards that do not meet the legislative criteria of a POCA. Examples include:

- paved or concrete exercise yards for dairy cows where no feeders or waterers are present
- winter feeding areas with a soil base for beef cows where the cows are present for less than 200 days per year
- corrals and livestock handling areas where livestock are not fed or watered.

A 'western-style' soil-floored beef finishing pen, complete with wind shelter fencing and a fence-line feeder

In these situations, the following rules apply:

- if the Regulation requires the farm to have a Nutrient Management Strategy (NMS), all nutrients must be managed according to the NMS.

- the handling of runoff from the paved livestock yard and POCA must follow Regulation, Sec. 81.
- a permanently vegetated area can only be used for runoff management on a paved livestock yard if the manure from the livestock has a dry matter of 30 per cent or greater as listed in the Nutrient Management Tables in the Regulation.

While the Regulation stipulates that manure and runoff from the winter-feeding areas listed above, as well as corrals and livestock handling areas must be managed, it does not specify how this must be done. It is the NMS that will outline how nutrients from these yards are to be managed in order to minimize any negative environmental effects.

The NMS should detail best management practices, proper siting recommendations (i.e. distance to surface water and wells) and other appropriate measures for the particular livestock yard.

Farm operators must be prepared to explain this to the Ministry of Agriculture, Food and Rural Affairs during approvals, or to Ministry of the Environment officials during inspection.

A Solid Base for Groundwater Protection

The Regulation does not require outdoor confinement areas or livestock yards to have concrete or paved floors. However, it is recommended. This allows:

- Easier collection of manure to later spread on fields that require nutrients
- Runoff to be directed to a proper area for management.

It is much easier on the operator, equipment and animals if a concrete or hard base is present in these areas, especially during wet periods.

Sensitive Features

New–or expanding–permanent outdoor confinement areas on farms with a NMS must be sited to ensure proper setbacks from sensitive features, including wells and field drainage tiles. Setback distances reduce the likelihood of manure or nutrients reaching watercourses and wells (Table 12.2). The distance must be measured from the closest point of animal access in the POCA to the setback feature.

Table 12.2: Setback Distances Required for POCAs

Water Source or Feature	Setback Distance Requirement
Drilled wells of 15 m (50 ft.) or more depth and water tight casing to a depth of 6 m (20 ft.) or more	15 m (50 ft.)
Other wells including oil, gas, and water, unused and test wells not meeting the above criteria	30 m (100 ft.)
Municipal wells	100 m (330 ft.)
Field drainage tiles	15 m (50 ft.)

If the runoff management includes using a permanently vegetated area, the flow path distance should be at least 150 m to surface water or tile inlet. The Regulation prohibits direct livestock access to surface water in some POCAs.

Runoff Control Requirements

Runoff from a livestock yard usually contains some manure. Runoff yields can range from 15 per cent to 50 per cent of precipitation and depend on storm intensity, pen slope, manure pack condition, stocking density as well as other factors.

The Regulation (sec. 81) lists the five acceptable runoff management systems allowed for permanent outdoor collection areas: roof and up-slope water diversion; runoff containment; vegetated filter strip systems; sewage works under the Building Code or Ontario Water Resources Act and permanently vegetated areas. These may be used separately or as a system.

1. *Roof and Up-Slope Water Diversion:* Reducing the amount of clean water entering the POCA is an acceptable runoff management method (Part VII, Regulation), along with roofing or permanently covering the area. One technique is to direct clean water from eaves troughs and gutters into non-perforated tile, berms or ditches.
2. *Runoff Containment:* A new or expanded runoff collection and storage system must meet the Siting and Construction Standards (Part VIII, Regulation) for liquid storage facilities. The choice of design (i.e. earthen lagoon or concrete tank) will determine the level of site investigation required.

Manure and Snow Removal and Storage

The Regulation, s. 60, allows a pen floor to be used to store manure. As a result, the NMS can allow manure to either be stored in the POCA for up to one year or placed in storage (temporary field storage or another permanent storage). It is possible to have the manure remain in the POCA for more than one year if it is declared in the NMS as part of a mounding system for animal management (resting areas). It may also be directly applied to land, or transferred to another farm unit, another farmer or a manure broker as with other manures and storages.

Snow and ice pack are a concern in livestock yards as the material is bulky and when it melts can lead to increased runoff volumes. Options for managing this 'feedlot snow' material include:

- Transferring to a manure storage facility.
- Transferring to a temporary field storage site, if the NMS permits a method for dealing with melt water runoff.
- Land application, if the material meets the parameters in Part 11 of the NM Protocol.
- There is a 40 m setback from the top of the bank.
- A minimum application setback of 60 m to a drilled well, 400 m to municipal well and 120 m to all other wells.
- The maximum slope of the field is three per cent.
- There is minimum 6 m vegetated buffer along all surface water in the field and.
- The manure is applied at an application rate of half of the normal maximum rate (i.e. if the normal rate of application is 36 tonnes/ hectare (16 tons/acre), then the rate for snow containing manure is 18 tonnes/hectare (8 tons/acre).

The Regulation does not specify requirements for applying snow-covered manure from livestock and wintering yards that do not meet the criteria of a POCA. Nor does it indicate requirements for mounding manure.

Producers with livestock yards and winter sites need to practice good management to avoid an adverse effect from the manure and runoff from these areas as well.

13 Road Drainage

With a rural road network drainage of the road pavement will mostly be just down to the maintenance of ditches adjacent to the highway, and ensuring that all culverts are free flowing, not complicated but it is surprising how often these simple maintenance procedures are neglected.

One must keep the water-table low below and surrounding the road pavement to prevent the moisture content of the subgrace increasing, and hence decreasing the subgrade strength.

A highway gully is a drainage pit covered by an open metal grating located on the road edge. It's purpose is to drain rain water from the three components of adequate road or track drainage are surface, side and cross drainage.

SURFACE DRAINAGE

Road Crowning

Crowning provides a low-grade fall enabling drainage from both sides of the centre of the road. This method is only effective if the crown is slightly higher than the natural surface.

Road Crowning Should be Avoided in Areas

Those places where water naturally crosses the road such as broad drainage floors. Floodways are required in these cases.

Infall and Outfall Drainage

When roads are built across the slope consideration must be given to taking water from the up slope side of the road to the down slope side of the road. When you install cross drainage you must make sure that it does not cause erosion of the road surface.

Crossfall/Outfall Drainage

The simplest method is by providing the road surface with a crossfall in the same direction as the slope (outfall drainage), thereby directing water over the road surface to disposal areas on the lower side of the road.

The other method is by providing the road surface with infall drainage back into the slope, directing water back to the up slope side of the road. If infall drainage is necessary then table drains, culverts or inverts need to be constructed. These will safely direct outfall drainage is preferred to infall drainage as there is generally no need for other drainage works such as culverts, inverts, table and mitre drains.

When installing outfall drainage on steeper slopes, batters on the downslope side of the road must not be too steep. Steep batters may erode, impacting on the road itself.

The crossfall of the road surface should be kept as flat as possible to ensure good drainage. For outfall drainage it is recommended that the maximum crossfall slope be in the order of 1.5 to 2 per cent, whereas in fall drainage slopes can be as great as 4 per cent water to the down slope side of the road.

SIDE DRAINAGE

Table Drains

Table drains are excavated open channels that are built parallel to roads and tracks. These drains direct runoff to disposal areas further downslope. Table drains should only be used when natural run-off is not possible.

Fill obtained from constructing table drains can be used to build up road surfaces. The design of table drains depends on a number of factors, including the size and nature of the catchment, the slope and water volumes and flow. Larger table drains may need to be designed by engineers or soil conservation officers. Table drains should be constructed with a flat bottom (trapezoid shape). In general they should be 0.5 to 1.0m wide at the base. Avoid using V-shaped drains as they may cause erosion in the channel.

Where possible table drains should be revegetated as soon as possible after construction, and regularly slashed.

Mitre Drains

Water should be taken out of table drains at regular intervals using mitre (offshoot) drains. Mitre drains take runoff out of table drains or directly off road shoulders where table drains are absent. These drains dispose of water in areas away from the road.

Mitre drains stop water accumulating in table drains or on the road shoulder. Ideally mitre drains should be constructed so that they have a broad flat base at least 1m wide. Mitre drains also should not be graded to produce a V. Mitre drains should slope to direct the flow of water away from the road. To minimise erosion the slope should be no greater than 0.5 per cent on erodible soils or 1 per cent on stable soils. Mitre drain outlets effectively concentrate runoff, for this reason they should be located in stable undisturbed areas.

Mitre drain spacing is dependent on:

- the grade of the table drain or road;
- soil type and erodibility; and
- rainfall.

CROSS DRAINAGE

Engineered, stable cross drainage such as inverts, floodways or culverts can be used to collect water from upslope table drains, or drainage lines. It is generally more economical and practical to ford drainage lines using floodways or inverts than to use major culverts or bridges. On steeper country, where creeks and drainage lines are deeper, culverts may be more practical.

Inverts and Floodways

Care must be taken in the design and construction of flood ways and inverts in order to cause minimal interference to natural flows.

Inverts and flood ways are designed to be temporarily over topped by water flow and minimise bank and bed erosion. They should be sited at low points in the bank and at right angles to the direction of flow.

Inverts

Inverts should be constructed with the finished surface at, or just below the level of the existing stream bed. Construction of an invert is generally based on excavating soft, erodible material. At least 300mm should be removed, geotextile may be necessary as a base.

Excavated material is then replaced with compacted granular material to provide a trafficable surface.

Floodways

Floodways are usually elevated above the bed level of the channel and often incorporate culverts to take "normal" flows with the road only being overtopped during flood events.

The design should have ends of the structure that are well anchored into the banks and obstruction to flow kept to a minimum by using gentle batter slopes on the up- and downstream faces. When it is necessary to construct an elevated floodway it is recommended that specialist advice be sought. As floodways are generally elevated above bed level protection works are required on the downstream side of the floodway to prevent erosion.

CULVERTS

When culverts are used they should be angled downward at between 1 and 3 per cent. This will minimise silting of the pipe and prevent excessive scouring at the outflow. On drainage lines the culvert should be keyed into the streambed by digging a trench and seating the culvert into it. The area below the outlet will need protection to prevent erosion. This protection can be achieved by armouring (eg: rock mattress) the drain downstream of the outlet, or by constructing a dissipating device.

Protection may also be required at the inlet. The location, spacing, size and type of culvert may vary. Advice should be sought from Soil Conservation Officers prior to construction.

WHOA BOYS ON VEHICLE TRACKS

Whoa boys can vary in size. They can be a couple of metres long and only 10–30cm high on walking tracks, or they may be large, gently sloping banks up to 30-40m and up to 3 m high on deeply eroded areas.

Whoa boys can be constructed in two ways:

1. By cut and fill –Lines are ripped across the area at a grade of 0.3 per cent. A shallow channel should be cut along this line.

Excavated material is dumped on the down slope side of the channel, then compacted and smoothed out to form a bank with even batters and a level top.

2. Using imported soil material to construct a bank with a grade of between 0.3 and 0.5 per cent along the up slope edge of the bank. To aid trafficability, an approach and departure ramp can be cut into the bank.

The bank should be run off into undisturbed vegetation or into an existing drain (care needs to taken to ensure that erosion does not occur where the water runs down into the drain).

Rainwater, which strains through the permeable surface and is absorbed by the structure supporting the road, will damage the stability of the road itself. In these cases, road drainage must be laid longitudinally along the roadway edge and in the centre of the traffic divider to remove water infiltrations.

It need operating so that the underground water is collected and eliminated by the drainage pipe, the only effective drainage road to guarantee permanent results.

Failure Due to Hydraulic Pressure

Once water has entered a road pavement, water damage is initially caused by hydraulic pressure, i.e. vehicles passing over the road pavement impart considerable sudden pressure on the water present in the road pavement, this pressure forces the water further into the road fabric and breaks it up, this process can be very rapid once it begins.

Water that has entered the road pavement and is subject to the process of freezing (expansion) and thawing during the winter also brings about the swift failure of the road pavement.

Eventually the water will descend to the subgrade layer below the road pavement and weaken this layer thus lowering the CBR of the subgrade which the road pavement design was based upon, and deep seated failure of the road will begin.

Failure Due to Binder Stripping

Most aggregates have a greater affinity for water than they do bitumen, and with the presence of water and movement of the aggregate it is quite possible for the binder film on the aggregate particle to be broken and water to come in to contact with the aggregate surface.

Once the integrity of the binder layer has been broken it will depend upon the chemical nature of the aggregate particle and the viscosity of the binder as to how long it will be before stripping of the aggregate particles becomes an engineering problem.

Depending on the viscosity of the binder and the thickness of the binder film surrounding the aggregate the stripping of the bitumen will occur hardly at all, fairly slowly or quite quite quickly.

This can be compared:

(*a*) to a film of highly viscous 50pen. grade bitumen enhanced with cellulose or mineral fibres which will create a thick stable coating of bitumen around the aggregate particle;

(*b*) a low viscosity, highly workable, low temperature, hand-lay cutback material for emergency patching or very low stress sites.

The second example strips quite readily, and in most cases should only be regarded as a temporary measure before being removed and a more stable bituminous material used to replace it.

There are many degrees of stripping between the two examples I quote, and it is a fact that some aggregate sources are more prone to stripping than others.

The more durable bituminous mixtures, i.e. hot rolled asphalt and stone mastic asphalt are designed and produced to have high bitumen contents with almost all voids filled with bitumen to provide an impervious matrix, that will be highly resistant to stripping.

With proprietary thin surface course systems (Thin Surfacings) surface courses (wearing courses), many of these surfacing materials will actually be designed to allow the passage of water through the material matrix.

And, even though they will contain penetration grade bitumens, because of their exposed position in the road pavement structure these porous bituminous mixtures will have increased exposure to water in the internal matrix of the material, and this will increase the potential rate of stripping of the bitumen.

The will be dependent upon thickness of binder film on the aggregate particles, this usually being closely related to the binder content of the bituminous mixture.

This is when the pavement has failed, maybe not completely, but in a major way.

The pavement is no longer able to absorb and transmit the wheel loading through the fabric of the road without causing fairly rapid further deterioration of the road pavement.

The layers making up the road pavement have failed for various reasons, but one of the most common is poor drainage, either by:

- Lack of adequate drainage provision in the original road pavement design.
- Lack of maintenance of the drainage so that it no longer functions in a correct manner and the water table has risen.thus weakening the road pavement.

- Failure of the impervious nature of the surface course (wearing course), or the binder course (basecourse) where the surface course is a porous textured material, thus allowing the passage of surface water in to the road pavement matrix.

Common Cause of Road Failures

Drainage is an important aspect of road construction and maintenance. e. It is of two types:

(*a*) Surface drainage; and

(b) subsurface drainage.

Surface drainage is collection of rain water from the surface of the road to side drains or to lower sides in open terrain.

It is possible if the road have sufficient cross slope about 2 per cent and free from depressions, potholes and cracks otherwise water will enter into the road structure. Subsurface drainage is collection of that water that has entered into the road structure.

Once water has entered a road pavement, water damage is initially caused by hydraulic pressure, i.e. vehicles passing over the road pavement pass on considerable sudden pressure on the water present in the road pavement, this pressure forces the water further into the road structure and breaks it up, this process can be very rapid once it begins.

Sooner or later, the water will descend to the subgrade layer below the road pavement and weaken this layer thus lowering the C.B.R. of the subgrade, and complex failure of the road will begin.

Binding Failure (Stripping of Aggregates)

Most aggregates have a greater affinity for water than bitumen, and with the presence of water and movement of the aggregate it is quite possible for the binder film on the aggregate particle to be broken and water to come in to contact with the aggregate surface.

Once the integrity of the binder layer has been broken it will depend upon the nature of the aggregates, viscosity and thickness of bitumen layer as to how long it will be before stripping of the aggregates.

The layers making up the road pavement have failed for various reasons, but one of the most common is poor drainage, either by :

1. Inadequate drainage provision in the original road pavement design.
2. Lack of maintenance of the drainage so that it no longer functions in a correct manner.

3. Rise in water table thus weakening the road pavement.
4. Failure of the impervious nature of the surface course such as thin layers of premix carpet without proper sealing coat, cracks and potholes and undulations causing pooling, thus allowing the passage of surface water in to the road pavement matrix.

14 Drainage Districts

Drainage districts occur in England and Wales, varying in size from a few hundred acres to over 100,000 acres (400 km^2), all in low lying areas of the country where flood risk management and land drainage are sensitive issues.

Most drainage districts are administered by an internal drainage board (IDB), which are single purpose local drainage authorities, dealing with the drainage and water level management of clean water only.

Each drainage district has a defined area, and the IDB only has powers to deal with matters affecting that area.

Drainage districts were also used in Chicago before the Tunnel and Reservoir Plan created underground reservoirs to hold storm water.

INTERNAL DRAINAGE BOARD

An internal drainage board (IDB) is a type of operating authority which is established in areas of special drainage need in England and Wales with permissive powers to undertake work to secure clean water drainage and water level management within drainage districts. The area of an IDB is not determined by county or metropolitan council boundaries, but by water catchment areas within a given region. IDBs are geographically concentrated in the Broads, Fens in East Anglia and Lincolnshire,Somerset Levels and Yorkshire. In comparison with public bodies in other countries, IDBs are most similar to the Waterschappen of the Netherlands, Consorzi di bonifica e irrigazione of taly, wateringenof Flanders and Northern France and watershed districts of Minnesota, USA.

Much of their work involves the maintenance of rivers, drainage channels (rhynes), ordinary watercourses, pumping stations and other critical infrastructure, facilitating drainage of new developments, the ecological conservation and enhancement of watercourses, monitoring and advising on planning applications and making sure that any development is carried out in line with legislation. IDBs are not responsible for watercourses designated as main rivers within their drainage districts; the supervision of these water-courses is undertaken by the Environment Agency.

History

Internal drainage boards date back to 1252; however, the majority of today's IDBs were established by national government following the passing of the Land Drainage Act 1930 and predominantly operate under the Land Drainage Act 1991 under which, an IDB is required to exercise a general supervision over all matters relating to water level management of land within its district.

Some IDBs may also have other duties, powers and responsibilities under specific legislation for the district (for instance the Middle Level Commissioners are also a navigation authority). IDBs are responsible to Defra from whom all legislation/regulations affecting them are issued. The work of an IDB is closely linked with that of the Environment Agency which has a range of functions providing a supervisory role over them.

Fundamental Role

The fundamental role of an internal drainage board is to manage the water level within its district. The majority of lowland rivers and watercourses have been heavily modified by man or are totally artificial channels. All are engineered structures designed and constructed for the primary function of conveying surplus run-off to their outfall efficiently and safely, managing water levels to sustain a multitude of land functions. As with any engineered structure it must be maintained in order to function at or near its design capacity. Annual or bi-annual vegetation clearance and periodic de-silting (dredging) of these rivers and watercourses is therefore an essential component of the whole life cycle of these watercourses.

Accommodating sustainability within the design and maintenance process for lowland rivers and watercourses has to address three essential elements:

- year round conveyance of flows;
- storage of flood peaks; and
- retention and protection of flora and fauna dependent on or resident in the water corridor.

Many IDBs are redesigning watercourses to create a two-stage or bermed channel. These have been extensively created in the Lindsey Marsh Drainage Board area of East Lincolnshire to accommodate the three elements of lowland watercourse sustainability.

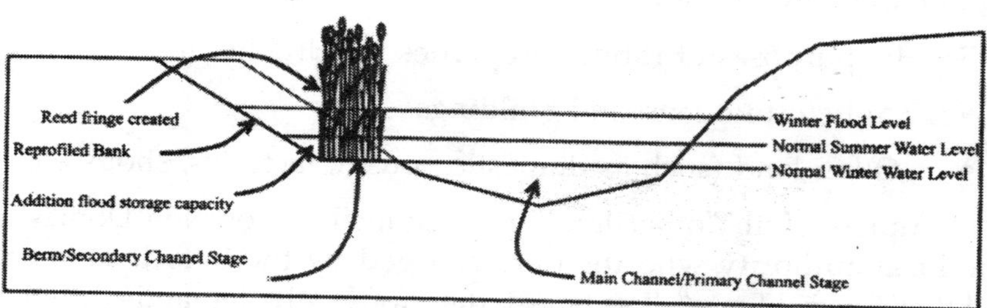

Fig. 14.1

Berms are created at or near to the normal retained water level in the system. It is sometimes replanted with vegetation removed from the watercourse prior to improvement works but is often left to re-colonise naturally. In all cases this additional part of the channel profile allows for enhanced environmental value to develop.

The area created above the berm also provides additional flood storage capacity whilst the low level channel can be maintained in such a manner that design conveyance conditions are achieved and flood risk controlled.

By widening the channel and the berm, the berm can be safely used as access for machinery carrying out channel maintenance. Whilst, in-channel habitat that develops can be retained for a much longer period during the summer months, flood storage is provided for rare or extreme events and a buffer zone between the channel and any adjacent land use is created.

The timing of vegetation clearance works is essential to striking a sustainable balance in lowland watercourses. The Conveyance Estimating System (CES) is a modelling tool developed through a Defra/Environment Agency research collaboration. IDBs use CES to estimate the seasonal variation of conveyance owing to vegetation growth and other physical parameters which they use to assess the impact of varying the timing of vegetation clearance operations.

This is critical during the Spring and early summer, the prime nesting season for aquatic birds, the breeding season for many protected mammal species such as water voles and the season when many rare species of plant life flower and seed. Many IDBs have developed vegetation control strategies in co-ordination with Natural England.

Drainage Rates

All properties within a drainage district are deemed to derive benefit from the activities of an IDB. Every property is therefore subject to a drainage rate paid annually to the IDB.

For the purposes of rating, properties are divided into:

- Agricultural land and buildings
- Other land (such as domestic houses, factories, shops etc).

Occupiers of all "other land" pay Council Tax or Non-Domestic Rates to the local authority who then are charged by the board. This charge is called the "Special Levy". The board, therefore, only demands drainage rates direct on agricultural land and buildings. The basis of this is that each property has been allotted an "annual value" which were last revised in the early 1990s. The annual value is an amount equal to the yearly rent, or the rent that might be reasonably expected if let on a tenancy from year to year commencing 1 April 1988. The annual value remains the same from year to year. Each year the board lays a rate "in the £" to meet its estimated expenditure. This is multiplied by the annual value to produce the amount of drainage rate due on each property.

Drainage districts are local bodies formed for the purpose of draining, ditching, and improving land for agricultural and sanitary purposes. They are authorized to build and maintain drains and levees, to sue all necessary private land within their corporate bodies for that purpose, and to tax land within their boundaries as necessary.

The Illinois Constitution of 1870 authorized the General Assembly to pass laws giving landowners drainage rights, including the use of adjoining land for ditching purposes. As a result, a comprehensive drainage law was passed in 1871. The law set up legal procedures for local citizens to petition the county courts for drainage works, assessing and collecting the costs of the drainage construction from the owners of the lands to be benefited by the work, and compensating the owners of land which would be entered for ditching purposes. The county courts were given authority to appoint three drainage commissioners; township commissioners of highways could also serve as drainage commissioners.

The 1871 law was found unconstitutional; as a result the Illinois Constitution was amended, making drainage commissioners the heads of corporate drainage districts and giving these districts constitutional authority to levy property taxes. Two separate and coequal Illinois drainage laws were passed in 1879. One, the "Levee Law," repeated the procedures of the 1871 law, with added procedures for legal appeal by landowners dissatisfied with their assessments; the second, the "Drainage District Law," made the township highway commissioners the township drainage district commissioners. For non-township-organized counties, the county commissioners served as drainage commissioners. For districts extending over three or more townships, districts were set up and temporary commissioners appointed by county courts, similarly to the "Levee Law," but if the drainage district contained more than 15 landowners, the owners elected the three commissioners. Both laws gave commissioners three-year terms. From 1871 to 1885, Illinois law required that all drainage commissions have three members· In 1885, drainage districts in which drainage construction had been completed were authorized to appoint only one commissioner. Although Illinois drainage law was recodified in 1955, the responsibilities of drainage commissioners have largely remained unchanged since 1871. From 1871 to the present, the commissioners have been required to file annual financial reports with the county or circuit courts.

Purpose of Drainage Districts

Drainage districts were established for drainage of surface waters from agricultural and other lands for the protection of said lands from overflow when said protection is a public benefit or is conducive to public health, convenience, and welfare (Section 468.2, State Code Of Iowa).

Districts are established by the Drainage District Trustees at the request of the land owners within the proposed district (Section 468.6-468.8). Petitions and actions to establish are kept in the minute books in the county courthouse.

Under the Code of Iowa, Chapter 468 the County Board Of Supervisor's act as Drainage District Trustees in all District matters. The landowners of a particular district may, if they wish, elect their own trustees and maintain the district themselves.

Requests for repairs, complaints, problems, or questions should be directed to Drainage District Clerk Paul Ketelsen at 563-659-8149 located in the Clinton County DeWitt Annex at 329 E. 11th St. DeWitt.

The trustees are required by the Code of Iowa to maintain all drainage districts at their original capacity. Notice of repairs is only required when the cost will exceed $15,000 or 75 per cent of the original assessed value of the district, whichever is greater.

Land owners in the district, not the County, own and pay for all maintenance and repairs to that district. A contractor hired by the trustees will do the work and bill the cost to the district.

Assessments are made as necessary to pay for engineering costs, improvements, and repairs within a given drainage district.

Assessments or classification of land in a drainage district is based on the benefit that land is seen to receive from being in the district.

- The original assessed value of any parcel of land within a district was set when that district was established and is the basis for all assessments unless the district is reclassified by the trustees.
- Assessments represent a per centage of the original assessment.
- Properties near the bottom of the district or adjacent to a district ditch or tile line will normally pay more than properties at the top of the district or that are not close to a district tile.

Drainage districts are not levied on a regular basis. Drainage districts are levied when district funds drop to zero. When a district is levied the trustees set the per centage such that a surplus remains after all bills are paid. The district will not be levied again until its funds are depleted which depends on the amount of work required in the district. Some districts are levied frequently while some may go 50 years or more without a levy.

Self-managed Irrigation and Drainage Districts

Self-financing Irrigation and Drainage Districts (SIDDs) in China are a type of PIM. To promote long-run sustainability, SIDDs emphasize self-financing. However, the basic principle behind both PIM and the SIDDs is that farmers should participate and have some management control in decisions which affect their future and livelihood. The SIDD concept or system has been developed in China to match Chinese conditions and deal with many of the key issues facing Chinese irrigation management. The SIDD system is also designed to incorporate and implement Chinese policies and reforms, like "market oriented" development, the "user pays" principle, treatment of water as a commodity, water charges to cover costs, water charges according to volume of water used to encourage efficient use, and direct participation and self-management by the water users who contribute to the investments.

To date, some 490 WUAs and 38 WSCs or WSOs (Water Supply Organizations) have been established in 10 provinces and three large municipalities including Beijing on a pilot basis, supported under six ongoing or proposed World Bank-financed projects. The results of these SIDD pilot projects have generally been positive, especially for the WUAs, with increased production, reduced water waste, increased water charge collections, reduction or elimination of water conflicts among farmers, and increased "ownership," participation and contributions by farmers.

A key challenge for the future of SIDD and WUA development will be how to maintain WUA quality as they spread to wider areas, when few

Water Resources staff have training in and experience with the participatory concepts on which their work with WUAs are based. A second key challenge will be how to overcome the internal government bureaucratic and institutional constraints faced by the WSCs or any type of WSO reform, which is essential to reform main system management. The need for this reform will become increasingly important in order to save water and provide high quality water supply to users, as the WUAs spread.

Index